Come Unto ME

BY R.L. MONTGOMERY

Come Unto ME
By R.L. Montgomery

Copyright © 2016 by R.L. Montgomery

All rights reserved. No portion of this publication may be reproduced, shared in any electronic system, or transmitted in any form or by any means, electronic, mechanical, photocopy, recording, or otherwise, without written permission from the author.

Edited by Richard M. Davis and Patricia Williams

Cover design and layout by Dennis Fiorini, Graphics Gourmet

All Scripture quotations are taken from the King James Version (KJV) of the Bible, unless otherwise specified. The New King James Version when quoted is given as (NKJV). Scripture taken from the New King James Version®. Copyright © 1982 by Thomas Nelson. Used by permission. All rights reserved.

The names of those mentioned in the book have been changed to protect their privacy.

Printed in the United States of America by Morris Publishing.

ISBN 978-0-692-78406-8

Printed in the United States by Morris Publishing®
3212 East Highway 30
Kearney, NE 68847
1-800-650-7888

DEDICATION

THIS testimony is dedicated to my brother who invited me to my first prayer meeting wherein I first believed. Because of his invitation I later received the beautiful baptism of the Holy Ghost. To my brother, Will, who later turned from the Holy Spirit to seek a deeper Catholic experience, and to the many others who attended the prayer meetings is this book written and dedicated. I pray they will return to seeking the guidance of the Holy Ghost and will allow Him to lead them into all truth.

"*Howbeit when he, the Spirit of truth, is come, he will guide you into all truth*" (John 16:13).

TABLE OF CONTENTS

Dedication	5
Preface	9
Acknowledgements	11
Turning Around	13
Spiritual Navigation: The Importance of God's Word	21
Set Free from Praying to Mary	27
Delivered from Further Idolatry	35
The Catholic View of Mary	39
Mary Needed a Savior	43
Breaking Away from the Catholic Church	51
The Old and New Testament Tabernacles	57
The Apostle Peter and Water Baptism	67
Living in the Power of the Spirit	79
Not Three Gods in One, but One God in Christ Jesus	83
Avoiding Common Misconceptions about Salvation	101
Full Salvation Enduring to the End	109
Index	119
Scripture Index	122

PREFACE

HAVE you ever reached a point in which life became puzzling and your mind was overrun by questions? I have. At the point in which this story begins, I had reached such a place and my heart was filled with questions. I had everything I wanted but was miserable inside. Many news articles and unusual weather patterns seemed to signal changing and uncertain times. I wondered if our world as we know it would possibly end during my lifetime and I began to question if I was prepared to meet the Lord for judgment. Would I really make it to Heaven?

Not knowing who to go to, my search for help began in bookstores. Searching the self-help section of bookstores, I hoped to find answers to my own countless questions. When I was unable to find my answers in the self-help areas, I turned to the religious book section for help. Troubled by seeming "loopholes" I was practicing in my Catholic faith, I was anxious to glean insights that would answer the burning questions in my heart. However, I was dismayed at what I found in some books written about Catholics. The books did not instruct Catholics how to do right but condemned them for their beliefs. Some of the books pointed out faults, but the books did not teach me how to get right with God. In addition, the tone in which the books were written lacked love or care for our fellow man. As Christians, the Scriptures command us to share the truth in a spirit of love by "speaking the truth in love" (Ephesians 3:15).

These experiences inspired me to attempt to share what I learned and experienced in my own search for truth, hopefully in a tone of love. In addition, I have tried to keep this book short for the ease of my readers. One could easily read the book in a short time, however, I do not suggest that. This book attempts to prepare every reader to humbly receive biblical correction where it is needed. As I personally learned in my effort to draw closer to God, His corrections initiate changes that often are uncomfortable and are difficult to accept. Consequently, I suggest reading the material slowly and prayerfully while humbly seeking to draw closer to God. In this book I share my own lessons of spiritual growth as I searched for truth. This testimony offers answers to all believers—and especially to Catholics—which can lead them to a closer personal relationship with the Mighty God in Christ Jesus.

        R.L. Montgomery

ACKNOWLEDGEMENTS

A word of special thanks is due to so many people who have touched my life. Special thanks are due to three sisters the Lord used to invite me to church. I'm very grateful for their invitation.

My heartfelt appreciation is given to the three sisters that asked me to put into print verses of Scripture they could share with their Catholic families. This testimony was written in response to their requests. I also give thanks to the sister who gave me my first King James Bible.

The Lord has given me many wonderful pastors over the years who have given me much needed correction and direction in my life. In my path, the Lord also has sent evangelists who were extremely sensitive to the leading of His Spirit. If they were not sensitive and obedient to the move of the Lord, I would not have progressed spiritually to the point of where I am today.

Most of all, I thank the Lord Jesus Christ for leading me out of a life of sin and into a vibrant, growing day-to-day relationship and life with God. The Lord has been so patient, loving, and kind with me. Thank You, God, for the gift of Yourself and for all You have done.

Chapter ONE
TURNING AROUND

EVERYTHING in my life seemed to be coming to a sudden halt. It seemed nothing I set my hand to do would turn out right—not at home and certainly not at work either. Turmoil beset me on every side. Conviction of the way I had been living my life had been growing in me for a solid year. Now, the conviction had turned to sorrow. It was a sorrow drugs and alcohol could not drown out no matter how hard I tried, and try I did.

As I tried to escape the conviction it increased even more. In tears I would come home from work and head straight for my bedroom where I would fall to my knees and cry out to God with all my heart. Kneeling beside my bed, thoughts of my life would pass before my eyes and I would ask God to forgive me. As I began to seek God's forgiveness, visions of every wrong I had ever done—every sin I had ever committed—flashed rapidly before my eyes like a film. In tears, I began to tell God I was sorry. I did not realize this was true repentance. Since the visions of my sins were appearing before me like movie clips, I knew God had all of my sins on record. So I sought Him and asked His forgiveness for each and every offense.

This process of repentance went on for hours every night. After about three or four weeks, the visions of my sins changed from being the wrongs I had committed to the wrongs others had committed against me. Again, one by one, every wrong done to me was as a slide show before my eyes as I forgave every person and every circumstance.

Come Unto ME

After about a month of repentance and forgiveness, I began trying to live in a way that would please God. However, to my dismay I discovered I was unable to do so. I recognized that through my own power I was unable to stop myself from committing many of the sins of which I had just repented. This is when I realized sin had a hold on me. The thought of this bondage troubled me, so back to my knees I went again in prayer. This time was different, however. I began to cry out to God with all my heart, asking Him to please save me from these sins. This entreaty went on nightly. Crying and praying, I asked God to deliver me from my dilemma because I couldn't help myself. Then my brother, Will, began calling me and inviting me to a Wednesday night prayer meeting at his Catholic church nearly sixty miles away.

At first I told Will, "No, I would not go." However, one time he called and said, "If you are praying at home for God to help you or to lead you, and I call you to invite you, don't you think God is trying to answer your prayer? You need to say, 'yes,' and come." So I went. After all, how did he know I was praying and asking God these things when I had not told a single soul?

At the prayer meeting, about twenty or thirty people were sitting in a circle. Some were holding hands while others held their arms high above their heads worshiping God. Then something unusual began to happen. These people began to utter sounds and words I had never heard. Some of them even said the same exact sounds and words in unison. I began to think this was bizarre and became indignant. My thoughts about this event were unpleasant.

One of the speakers began speaking loudly in a different language and could be heard above all the others. Suddenly, they all went quiet and a solemn hush came across the room. Then instantly, the silence was broken by another voice, this time in English words I could understand. I bowed my head and cried because the spoken

Turning Around

words reflected all my negative thoughts about what I was witnessing. The message was boldly spoken (word for exact word), which mirrored my exact thoughts. I fell on my face in their midst and repented of all my doubts and negative thoughts. This experience was the hour I first believed. I knew then God was present in the prayer meeting for only He could have known my very thoughts. Years later I noticed this verse of Scripture:

> *If therefore the whole church be come together into one place, and all speak with tongues, and there come in those that are unlearned, or unbelievers, will they not say that ye are mad? But if all prophesy, and there come in one that believeth not, or one unlearned, he is convinced of all, he is judged of all: and thus are the secrets of his heart made manifest; and so falling down on his face he will worship God, and report that God is in you of a truth* (I Corinthians 14:23–25).

Soon the Elder who was leading the prayer group laid hands on me. Like the others, I too began speaking in tongues while worshiping and praising God. The experience was breathtaking. My heart was filled with so much love and joy from Jesus Christ I thought I was in Heaven. After an eternity-filled fifteen minutes, I felt like a new-born person. My heart felt so clean inside. My journey with the Lord had just begun. After this encounter I was drawn to read the Holy Bible in the privacy of my own home. I spent countless hours praying and reading my Bible. I felt so drawn to the Word of God I would weep and cry as I read the pages. Then, something began to happen; a verse of Scripture began to stand out to me. It was a verse in the Book of Hebrews that deals with a father correcting his child:

> *"My son, do not despise the chastening of the Lord, nor be discouraged when you are rebuked by Him; for whom*

> the Lord loves He chastens, and scourges every son whom He receives." If you endure chastening, God deals with you as with sons; for what son is there whom a father does not chasten? But if you are without chastening, of which all have become partakers, then you are illegitimate and not sons *(Hebrews 12:5–8, NKJV).*

These verses concerning correction and of being God's child kept coming back to me. I began to think possibly I was not receiving God's correction. In a simple prayer to the Lord, I said, "God, if I am Your child as You say I am because I have received the Holy Ghost, then won't You please correct me?" I wanted to feel correction so badly so I too could feel I was His child. I wanted to feel corrected so I could feel loved of the Lord as the Scripture stated. I'm so thankful God heard this simple prayer.

Unfortunately, a while after receiving the Holy Spirit, I began to seek a deeper Catholic experience. I was unaware God soon would begin correcting my Catholic traditions and practices. In reflection, I'm so thankful God was kind and merciful to correct me and to lift me up out of the pit of my sins. He delivered me from sins I did not know were sins. This book is a testimony and witness of multiple corrections God began to make in my life. He began to correct many practices or doctrines of the Catholic faith I had known from my childhood for I had returned and recommitted myself to them. I had no idea at the time of my prayer these Catholic practices were the doctrines and beliefs the Lord would correct.

Prior to the Lord's correcting me, He sent a person to cross my path. The vessel the Lord chose to administer His correction in my life was a wonderful Christian woman who also was a former Catholic. Her name is Terry. She once confided in me the Lord had laid it on her heart to witness to a particular person, but she did not do

Turning Around

it. Later the person died. This person was her Catholic grandmother. Terry was so grieved she had not witnessed to her grandmother that she vowed to the Lord never again to miss an opportunity to witness to a person when the Lord was leading her to do so. Terry's promise played a significant role in my life. Because of her desire to obey God, the Lord helped Terry greatly and gave her boldness in witnessing to me.

I admired Terry's great qualities of wisdom and patience both in her efforts to witness to others of her faith and also when she was suffering through her own trials. I came to realize how much I, too, needed those qualities to help me when I was suffering through similar trials as God was correcting me. I've observed others trying to correct a Catholic only to see it end in a heated debate. However, Terry never allowed me to draw her into an argument. What stood out most to me was that Terry always remained calm and had a peace about her even through the storms. Terry's patience gave me a feeling she was somehow different. She had a special way of bringing issues out into the open so we could discuss and deal with them.

Terry would ask me to pray, to lead in prayer, or to sing a song. She would even ask, "What has God done for you lately?" She was even bold enough to ask, "What has Mary done for you lately?" Then she would firmly and calmly say to me, "God does not like what you are doing. You need to quit that." If she could find it at the time, she would open her Bible and show me the Scripture verse dealing with the exact issue I had practiced or verbalized. If she perceived I could not handle correction at that time, she would approach me later in the day with the exact verse of Scripture I needed. Often she would just lay her Bible down and keep her finger on the Scripture verse saying, "Read this." Then she would walk away and leave me there with her Bible, allowing God to deal with me privately. If I gave her a reproach or endeavored to argue, she never returned in kind. Overall, her best tactics were the times when she would silently leave me alone and allow God to deal with me through His Word. After all, the Bible speaks of the power of God's Word.

> *For the word of God is quick, and powerful, and sharper than any two edged sword, piercing even to the dividing asunder of soul and spirit, and of the joints and marrow, and is a discerner of the thoughts and intents of the heart* (Hebrews 4:12).

This verse of Scripture describes what was happening to me on the inside as Terry was revealing to me God's will through His Word. One by one, I felt God tearing down the walls of my former practices that were displeasing Him. This process was not easy to go through. Change can sometimes be painful. However, I now can see the rewards are well worth enduring God's correction. I've experienced the fire of many corrections from God, so I can look back and recognize the positive good they have brought about in my life. I am eternally grateful for all God has taught me, even though it often was painful and difficult at the time. Further, God is not finished working on me. I encourage anyone reading my testimony to be strong and faithful because discovering and endeavoring to fulfill God's will is worth the pain and effort. As the Lord revealed to me in His Word just prior to starting this journey, we must "not despise the chastening of the Lord" or "be discouraged when . . . rebuked by Him." His correction is for our ultimate good.

If you are a Catholic reading this book and you feel the Word of God gripping your heart as well, remember that God loves you. As a loving Father, one way God deals with us is through His Word. His chastening, or correction was something I wanted because I wanted to experience His love for me. To know God loves us is one thing,

Turning Around

but to come into contact with His love is another thing altogether. To experience the love of God is to know

Him. I had asked God for Him to allow me to experience His love, which He revealed to me through loving correction.

The second correction God began to work in me involved another verse of Scripture I had read, which cut into my heart.

> *I marvel that ye are so soon removed from him that called you into the grace of Christ unto another gospel: Which is not another; but there be some that trouble you, and would pervert the gospel of Christ (Galatians 1:6–7).*

When I read this verse, the knowledge of the possibility of turning from the Lord "unto another gospel" haunted me. I felt as if the Lord was telling me I had received the Holy Ghost but I was turning from Him to seek something else. I didn't want to be removed from Him. I wanted to be closer to God. However, I could not understand what I was doing wrong or what it was I was turning to. God was preparing me so He could show me through His Word and by the witness of Terry that my idolatry was displeasing Him. I had not learned this lesson yet, but I didn't want to displease the Lord.

I had only received the Holy Spirit about six months prior and I was totally head-over-heels in love with the Lord. Still, these verses of Scripture were leading me to sense something I was doing was wrong; something was displeasing the Lord. Since God had given me the Holy Ghost in the Catholic Church, I had erroneously begun to think the doctrines and practices of Catholicism were okay; however, God was trying to reveal to me they were unacceptable. When a person's practices violate the Word of God, his or her life insults God. In seeking a deeper Catholic experience, I was slowly drifting away from God without noticing it. However, God noticed

Come Unto ME

I was shifting my love from Him, and He was reaching for me and endeavoring to deliver me from my erroneous ideas.

I invite you to read my testimony and share my experiences as God lovingly and beautifully corrected me and led me into a deeper relationship with Him. The Scriptures in the following chapters were monumental to me. As the Lord tore down the walls of false doctrine, I was able to see my need for salvation.

First, however, it seems important to consider the vital position of God's Word, the Bible, in all our lives. It is the essential roadmap to life, salvation, and eternal life in Heaven.

CHAPTER TWO
SPIRITUAL NAVIGATION:
THE IMPORTANCE OF GOD'S WORD

AS humankind began to create a means of traveling from one point to another, it was not long before they built seagoing vessels and began to venture out into the seas of the earth. At first, navigators remained near to land so they would have reliable "landmarks" and to ensure they did not become lost. They needed some kind of fixed markers they could rely on not to move—not to change positions. Only by observing these fixed landmarks could they navigate reliably on the open waters of the earth.

Eventually, navigators began to make charts of the waters and known landmarks from which explorers who would follow could navigate the same seas. In daylight hours they also were able to utilize the position of the sun, and at night they could use the moon. However, these celestial bodies were not stationary; they are bodies that travel across the horizons of our skies due to the continual rotation of the earth on its axis, as well as the changing of the four seasons. These celestial bodies help navigators, but allowances have to be made for their changing positions in the visible sky.

The navigators eventually came to recognize the invaluable navigational reference point provided by the North Star, Polaris. The North Star could function as a virtually unchanging landmark for navigators, allowing them to comfortably venture farther and farther away from land, and making it possible for them to explore the vast oceans and large seas of the earth.

Come Unto ME

> *The reason the North Star is so important for natural navigation is that it sits directly over the North Pole. Something that people often forget is that whenever you are trying to find true north, you are actually trying to find the direction of the North Pole from wherever you are (http://www.naturalnavigator.com, accessed March 19, 2015).*

In the same way explorers utilize the North Star, sun, moon, and landmarks in order to determine "true north" or to pinpoint their location for accurate navigation, and to avoid becoming lost, so spiritual explorers need an unchanging marker for spiritual navigation. For the spiritual traveler, the Bible—God's Word—is "true north." In other words, it is the reliable, unchanging point of reference to determine right from wrong, true from untrue, and holy from unholy.

The Bible is vital to every believer who desires salvation. There are at least four reasons why we desperately need the navigational guidance of God's Word in our lives.

(1) First, it is an unchanging point of spiritual reference. Mankind can come up with all sorts of ideas about religion, spirituality, or right and wrong, but there must be some unchanging reference to which one can point that will distinguish between correct ideas and wrong ideas. That reference point is the Word of God. This is why the Bible is so important to every one of us.

Without the Bible we have no way of determining right from wrong; we have no way to comprehend what is truth.

Pilate asked the immortal question centuries ago: "What is truth?" (John 18:38). Jesus boldly declared, "I am the way, the truth, and the life: no man cometh unto the Father, but by me" (John 14:6). Since Jesus Christ, God Incarnate, is "the truth," and since the Bible is the Word of God, then the Bible also must be the truth—a reliable,

Spiritual Navigation: The Importance of God's Word

unchanging, source of what is true and what is untrue. Further, Jesus said, "Search the scriptures; for in them ye think ye have eternal life: and they are they which testify of me" (John 5:39). Hence, Jesus Christ and the Word of God are an inseparable source of eternal truth. They never change and they are reliable as a consistent point of reference for navigating the seas of life—all the way to Heaven.

All scripture is given by inspiration of God, and is profitable for doctrine, for reproof, for correction, for instruction in righteousness (II Timothy 3:16).

Being born again, not of corruptible seed, but of incorruptible, by the word of God, which liveth and abideth for ever. For all flesh is as grass, and all the glory of man as the flower of grass. The grass withereth, and the flower thereof falleth away: But the word of the Lord endureth for ever. And this is the word which by the gospel is preached unto you (I Peter 1:23–25).

For ever, O Lord, thy word is settled in heaven (Psalm 119:89).

For the Lord is good; his mercy is everlasting; and his truth endureth to all generations (Psalm 100:5).

(2) Second, the Word of God shows us the way to God and how to experience a vibrant relationship with Him. The Bible gives us instruction and guidance for life. It shows us vital principles for discovering and experiencing spiritual fulfillment.

Thy word is a lamp unto my feet, and a light unto my path (Psalm 119:105).

(3) Third, God's Word reveals to us how to be saved and make Heaven our eternal home and destiny. Following the Word of God is

the only way we can discover how to live in a way that pleases God, which will draw us closer to Him in a redemptive relationship. Consequently, we, like the psalmist, should hide God's Word in our heart. "Wherewithal shall a young man cleanse his way? by taking heed thereto according to thy word. With my whole heart have I sought thee: O let me not wander from thy commandments. Thy word have I hid in mine heart, that I might not sin against thee" (Psalm 119:9–11).

(4) Fourth, God's Word is the pattern against which we must evaluate and measure our traditions. There is nothing wrong with spiritual traditions; they exist in every culture on earth. However, it is vital we subject our human traditions to the light and scrutiny of God's Word. It is the only way to ensure our traditions do not violate God's Word and condemn us.

> *Making the word of God of none effect through your tradition, which ye have delivered: and many such like things do ye* (Mark 7:13).

It would be a shame to go through life believing our actions and traditions were bringing honor to God only to discover in the end that we were dishonoring Him through unbiblical traditions. If we sincerely love God and desire salvation, we should have no qualms about relegating all our decisions, actions, and traditions to the holy Word of God.

To live life without the guidance of God's Word, hoping to be saved and make Heaven our home, would be akin to trying to take a road trip without a map or some type of guidance system. We may think we know how to get to our destination, and we may know others who think they know how to get there, but without guidance we are only guessing—and ultimately, we are sure to be lost and fail to find our way to the anticipated and desired destiny.

Spiritual Navigation: The Importance of God's Word

Reading and studying God's Word, on the other hand, provides the essential direction and guidance necessary for us to honor God in all we do and ultimately reach Heaven. Those who desire God's approval must study the Bible, correctly interpret it, and learn from its communicated truths.

Study to shew thyself approved unto God, a workman that needeth not to be ashamed, rightly dividing the word of truth (II Timothy 2:15).

Reading, studying, and memorizing the Bible should be a discipline in every sincere believer's life. If we value our relationship with God, desire to honor and please Him in all we do, and ultimately desire eternal salvation, God's Word should have a place of supreme importance in our lives and we should spend time with it—and with Him—in daily reading, study, and prayer.

The powerful Word of God and my desire for truth in my life opened the door for a relationship of Bible study and learning with my new friend, Terry. Further, the study of God's Word with Terry began to lead me along a path of understanding, challenge, and change. Recognizing the importance of the Word of God will help you to understand the context of my spiritual journey in which I sought to ensure I was living in truth according to the Scriptures.

I will now endeavor to share with you my journey toward and into all the truths of Scripture.

Come Unto ME

CHAPTER THREE
SET FREE FROM PRAYING TO MARY

WHEN I was a practicing Catholic people would ask why I was praying to Mary. My trained response was, "We pray to Mary and Mary prays for us to Jesus just like when you ask a friend to pray to Jesus for you." Later, I discovered this answer was not scriptural. Before I discovered it was unbiblical, it never occurred to me we do not pray to our friends, neither do we pray to the deceased.

Meanwhile, I continued praying to Mary and gradually was drawn deeper into the practice. Eager to learn more, I began to buy books about Mary. These books claimed Mary to be the co-Redemptrix, Mediatrix, and Advocatrix of the human race. This claim, which views Mary as having a mediating role alongside Christ, is a major root of Catholicism, which essentially and practically places Mary in a position equal with God. However, I was about to learn that praying to Mary and giving her thanks for things God had done was very displeasing to the Lord.

I did not realize that praying to Mary, singing songs to her, and thanking her for what I thought to be answered prayer was worship. I did not know the prayer wherein I asked for the Lord's chastening would lead me to embark on a journey that the Holy Spirit could use to change my life. The Lord wasted no time. The change began to get underway within a few days.

Terry approached me at work, stating she had heard I lived out near her and she needed someone with whom she could carpool to work. Immediately, I thought of how I loved being in my sports car and driving fast when I could, with my Christian music blasting. She told me she had a little baby girl and was trying to make ends meet. Loving children, I wanted to help her. Since I had a sports car we agreed to go in her car and that I would help her with the gas. Little did I know the Lord had me right where He wanted me.

There was more I soon would learn about Terry. I did not know she was filled with the Holy Ghost. I was also to discover she was a former Catholic. At times I did wonder why she walked into the building and onto the floor where I worked when she worked in an entirely different building. At the time, I simply shrugged it off thinking, *word gets around*. Later I was to see that our Lord was exhibiting His mercy and compassion for me through Terry. He was sending her to me so He could start me walking in the right path.

Terry and I began sharing our ride to work. The first few weeks we became acquainted with each other. During this time I learned that Terry was short for Theresa. She had stated she would not go by her former Catholic name. Terry had been raised a Roman Catholic in the same way I had been. She told me that when she was a young teenager she began to ask the Lord about the Catholic doctrines and to ask God to show her the truth. The Lord led her to a Christian church where she received the baptism of the Holy Ghost as evidenced by speaking in other tongues. In her young walk with the Lord, Terry stated she continued to ask God questions about her former Catholic teaching and asked the Lord to reveal to her the right ways from the Bible. She began to share with me some of what the Lord had taught her. However, she did not share these lessons in calm, sit-down, table-talk discussions. She would allow the Lord to bring my deep feelings to the surface, allowing for a much greater impact of scriptural teaching.

To bring my Catholic prayers out into the open, Terry used a subtle tactic. In her wisdom she would ask me to lead in prayer. Asking me to pray revealed to her what I was practicing in private. Then she would alert me to biblical errors I was making in my prayers. She would calmly state God did not like what I was doing, and she would show me Scripture for it. If she could not find the Scripture verse at the time, she would tell me she would find it and show me later. The next time we were together she would bring her King James Version Bible, place her finger under the Scripture, and ask me to read it.

Often I was frustrated and wanted to end my friendship with Terry because the Lord's chastening was unpleasant. However, I knew God had brought us together because He kept reminding me of my prayer requesting His chastening. Deep down I loved and respected Terry and still do to this day.

After getting acquainted, Terry invited me to a Christian prayer meeting at work. Their way of praying was so different from mine. The people prayed directly to God. As a Catholic, I had been taught I had to go through a saint because humans were too lowly to talk with God directly. Wow! These people were different from what I had been accustomed to, and it puzzled me. I also noticed they gave thanksgiving and praise directly to God. But I was still me—the Catholic! Once I got into the prayer group, I would slip up and mention a saint or statue. The other Christians would politely tolerate me and my Catholic mannerisms, but not Terry. She'd pull me aside and teach me regarding what I was doing wrong. She gave me verses of Scripture to support what she was telling me. Then, one day, I really *messed* up. One of my Catholic beliefs, which I really needed to get right with God, suddenly surfaced. It occurred while I was still a practicing Catholic.

Terry and I were driving home from work when I began to tell her of the "wonderful things Mary was doing in my life." Also, I began to explain to her how Mary is the "Mediatrix." Terry's jaw dropped.

She was stunned at what I was telling her. Then, suddenly, I began to feel the unpleasant correction of the Lord from the Holy Spirit. It was as if I could feel the Lord's anger upon me. I'd never felt God really angry at me before, so the Lord had my full attention.

Terry began to tell me how God does not give His glory or credit to another for things He has done. She also told me to look up the word *mediator* in my Bible when I was home. She told me I was using words I really didn't know the meaning of. She was right. When I was home, I ran upstairs and grabbed my Bible and my dictionary. Opening my dictionary first, I tried to look up the word *mediatrix*. My dictionary stated, "a feminine form of *mediator*, see *mediator*." Next, I looked up *mediator*. The definition of *mediator* stated, "a go-between between two opposing sides." Then it dawned on me the Bible teaches us that our Mediator is Jesus!

The Holy Ghost brought a verse of Scripture in the New Testament to my mind about the Mediator, a verse I had recently read but had not understood. I grabbed my Bible and looked it up. "For there is one God, and one mediator between God and men, the man Christ Jesus" (I Timothy 2:5).

I broke down, cried, and repented before the Lord. This correction taught me that Mary and the other saints cannot intercede for us. Never again did I pray to Mary or to any of the other saints. I learned that Jesus is my Mediator and High Priest. Only Jesus can intercede for us. The Lord was setting me free with the truth of His Word. To my amazement other verses of Scripture also deal with these simple basics and truths of having a relationship with Him. Hebrews 12:24 is another witness: "And to Jesus the mediator of the new covenant, and to the blood of sprinkling, that speaketh better things than that of Abel."

Set Free from Praying to Mary

Another verse of Scripture confirmed to me that only Jesus is able to intercede for me, and not any other:

> *By so much was Jesus made a surety of a better testament. And they truly were many priests, because they were not suffered to continue by reason of death. But this man, because He continueth ever, hath an unchangeable priesthood. Wherefore He is able also to save them to the uttermost that come unto God by him, seeing He ever liveth to make intercession for them* (Hebrews 7:22–25).

Not only does this verse mention Jesus being our intercessor, but it also points out Jesus is our Priest. Being raised a Catholic, I knew what it was like to have a priest. So these beautiful words of His priesthood really ministered to me and touched my heart. Hebrews 4:14 also mentions Jesus as our Priest:

> *Seeing then that we have a great high priest, that is passed into the heavens, Jesus the Son of God, let us hold fast our profession.*

Jesus did not teach His disciples to pray to Mary or to pray to other people. Instead, Jesus taught His followers to pray to the heavenly Father in His name.

> *Verily, verily, I say unto you, Whatsoever ye shall ask the Father in my name, he will give it you. Hitherto have ye asked nothing in my name: ask, and ye shall receive, that your joy may be full* (John 16:23–24).

When I read the above verse, it was as if a light bulb came on in my head. Suddenly I realized, *This is why the Christians pray differently from the way I had been taught to pray.* Soon God began working on my heart with other things I was not doing properly. The Lord needed to correct me in the way I gave God's glory to others instead of giving that glory to God in whom the praise was deserved. I did this by giving praise, worship, and thanks to the saints after my prayer was answered. I learned this lesson through Terry's help. Beginning to open up with Terry, she showed me a verse of Scripture that shows how God feels about worship: "For thou shalt worship no other god: for the LORD, whose name is Jealous, is a jealous God" (Exodus 34:14). This verse of Scripture is one the Lord gave Moses just prior to the second time He gave Moses the Ten Commandments. The Lord had taught Moses and the ancient Israelites not to worship anyone or anything but God alone. We must not give God's glory to any other.

> I the LORD have called thee in righteousness, and will hold thine hand, and will keep thee, and give thee for a covenant of the people, for a light of the Gentiles; To open the blind eyes, to bring out the prisoners from the prison, and them that sit in darkness out of the prison house. I am the LORD: that is my name: and my **glory will I not give to another, neither my praise to graven images** (Isaiah 42:6–8).

This passage of Scripture confirmed to me that God wants His people to have a relationship with Him. God taught me not to pray to Mary, the saints, or to give praise to others that belonged to God for things He had done.

Many years later I was to learn more clearly about the errors of how I had been taught as a child to pray to Mary and the saints. The Catholic nuns taught us to pray to Mary by using the miracle at the wedding feast at Cana. The Sunday school teacher at my new church brought out the true meaning behind the wedding feast at Cana.

Set Free from Praying to Mary

> *And the third day there was a marriage in Cana of Galilee; and the mother of Jesus was there: And both Jesus was called, and his disciples, to the marriage. And when they wanted wine, the mother of Jesus saith unto him, They have no wine. Jesus saith unto her, Woman, what have I to do with thee? mine hour is not yet come. His mother saith unto the servants, Whatsoever he saith unto you, do it* (John 2:1–5).

The nuns used this conversation between Mary and Jesus to erroneously teach us that Mary told Jesus what to do. By misusing this Scripture, we were taught to pray to Mary, and we were told she intercedes for us.

Now, my Sunday school teacher was teaching this lesson, and interestingly, he repeated the lesson three times. Each time my mind went back to what I was taught as a Catholic. Finally, the teacher asked me, "Sister, do you have some input here?" I responded, "All I know is what the Catholics taught me about this passage. I've always wondered what this really means." After the lesson was over, one of the elder brothers pulled me aside to instruct me that Mary never pointed the way to herself, but instead pointed the way to Christ. He said Mary guided them to do as "Jesus told them to do," **not what she told them to do**. He further explained to me that Mary never took God's glory unto herself.

God had taught me not to pray to Mary and the saints as well as to not give them praise. Earlier in this chapter I shared a verse of Scripture about not giving God's glory to graven images. Unfortunately, that was something I still was doing. I will share this with you in the next chapter.

Come Unto ME

CHAPTER **FOUR**
DELIVERED FROM FURTHER IDOLATRY

THE giving of God's glory to others and the idolatry I was practicing involved more than only praying to Mary. My practice of idolatry was intermeshed into other beliefs and actions. As mentioned earlier in this testimony, after about six months of walking with God, He began correcting my unbiblical practices. I had recently stopped praying to the saints but was having difficulty understanding exactly what the Lord expected from me. Shamefully, I admit I was slow to learn. I was still getting on my knees to pray to God, however, I was still praying in front of statues or pictures. This habit was part of my custom, and the idols remained in my home. I began reading my Bible about what I was practicing and seeking to discover what the Lord desired.

In my search the Lord began leading me to read the Old Testament Scriptures. While reading the Book of Deuteronomy, I came across the Ten Commandments in full, not realizing as a child we were given a shortened version of the Ten Commandments. Reading the full version of the Ten Commandments for the first time spoke greatly to my heart. The commandments convicted me of my style of praying and also brought me back to my third-grade class memories with the nun who gave me most of my early Catholic training.

In this third-grade class, I could remember being taught part of the Ten Commandments from Deuteronomy 5:7–8: "Thou shalt have none other gods before me. Thou shalt not make thee any graven image." I can remember going to my Catholic nun and asking her,

"Doesn't this mean we are not to get down on our knees to pictures and statues?" She responded:

"The statue or the picture is only to help us to focus on the being we are praying to and that is interceding to God on our behalf. So you see, we are not praying to the picture or to the statue. Instead, we are praying to the being who is in Heaven. You must remember this as it will help you to realize our prayers are not idolatry."

As an eight-year-old child, I can remember walking away from her and believing her. However, now I was an adult with the Holy Spirit and reading the full scriptural text of the Ten Commandments. In doing so, it was clear to me my style of praying to God in front of a statue or picture was indeed idolatry and was displeasing the Lord. Notice the full context of Exodus 20:3–6:

> *Thou shalt have no other gods before me. Thou shalt not make unto thee any graven image, or any likeness of any thing that is in heaven above, or that is in the earth beneath, or that is in the water under the earth. Thou shalt not bow down thyself to them, nor serve them: for I the* LORD *thy God am a jealous God, visiting the iniquity of the fathers upon the children unto the third and fourth generation of them that hate me; And shewing mercy unto thousands of them that love me and keep my commandments.*

The truth was undeniably and clearly right in front of me in the text of the Scriptures. Clearly, God does not want us kneeling or bowing to pictures and statues. This is when I realized the Catholic nun responsible for teaching me had deceived me as a child, whether by intention or by her lack of knowledge. Then I found another similar verse in Exodus 20:5, which I received as a confirmation: "Thou shalt not bow down thyself to them, nor serve them." By now, I had

Delivered from Further Idolatry

stopped praying to Mary, the saints, pictures, and statues, and I had begun seeking God with all my heart.

Suddenly there was a change in my prayers the following week. When I would try to pray, I began to weep and cry. The tears would not stop rolling off my face. Finally, at the end of the week, I fell to my knees crying to the Lord. The Holy Ghost came upon me strongly, and speaking softly to me asked, "What is troubling you?" I answered the Lord saying,

"Lord God, I am not crying because I miss those things (meaning the idol worship), but I'm crying because for the first time in my life I realize I don't know how to pray to You. All I know is my memorized prayers. Please, will You help me? Please, will You teach me?"

I remembered reading in the Scriptures something about "how the heathen" pray their repetitious prayers, and I didn't want the Lord to think of me as a heathen. I was totally in love with God by now and wanted to please Him.

When I was a practicing Catholic praying to the Lord, I was merely reciting (or reading to Him) prayers from a Catholic prayer book. Then I discovered Matthew 6:7: "But when you pray, use not vain repetitions, as the heathen do: for they think that they shall be heard for their much speaking." Because of this verse of Scripture, I did not want to merely recite someone else's prayer.

The Lord began to teach me to pray. He taught me I could simply speak to Him like my best friend. I learned this while reading in Isaiah where it states: "'Bring forth your strong reasons,' says the King of Jacob" (Isaiah 41:21, NKJV). This verse of Scripture in Isaiah caused me to think I could just talk to God. What He taught me was so sweet, so rewarding, and so satisfying to my soul that I thought to myself, *So this is what Christians mean by their words of "being able to have a walk with Him."*

Continuing my search on learning how to pray and seek God correctly, I read Psalm 119:2: "Blessed are those who keep His testimonies, who seek Him with the whole heart." In essence, the Lord was teaching me I could come directly to Him and pour my heart out to Him in prayer.

In addition, when we have needs we go to our heavenly Father in prayer and ask Him while calling on the name of Jesus. For example, Jesus said, "And whatsoever ye shall ask in my name, that will I do, that the Father may be glorified in the Son. If ye shall ask any thing in my name, I will do it" (John 14:13–14). My prayers took on the nature of simply talking to God with what was on and in my heart, thanking Him for anything He had done for me, and finished by asking God for any needs in Jesus' name.

After learning these various aspects about prayer, I believed He had opened my understanding. Thankful for His corrections, I looked up toward Heaven in prayer and said to Him, "Finally, Someone I can trust, and Someone I can love." God began teaching me to be diligent in giving prayers, worship, and thanksgiving to God only.

CHAPTER FIVE
THE CATHOLIC VIEW OF MARY

FROM the time I was a child, I was taught Mary was holy, pure, and always a virgin; she never died; and she ascended into Heaven on the clouds as our Lord did. We celebrated the feast of the "Ascension of Mary." I also was taught that Mary was both the mother of the human body of Christ and the mother of God Himself. To be the mother of God would elevate her above her status as human to a place of deity. These words also suggest she is equal to, or possibly even greater than God. It is so important for all Catholics not to view Mary in this false light. I later learned she was created as a person like you or me. She was created by God in the hope of her being obedient to God's will. Mary was obedient, but our reverence for and appreciation of her should end there. As the Lord had taught me, Mary is not my mediator nor will she ever be. She needed salvation as do we all.

Catholics believe Mary remained a virgin even after Jesus' birth. This false doctrine may not seem like a major issue or important to some, but it really is. This belief is an important issue that leads many individuals to worship her, which is idolatry. Mary's supposed virginity after giving birth to Jesus (not just before, but also after) is the basis for Catholics to worship her. We were taught in the Catholic Church that Joseph never "knew" her. This explains why Catholics teach that Mary is without sin. By the age of seven I was taught that Mary and Joseph never had any other children. My friend Terry knew my beliefs because she had been taught the same thing. The following are the first verses of Scripture Terry showed me regarding these ideas:

> *Then Joseph being raised from sleep did as the angel of the Lord had bidden him, and took unto him his wife: And knew her not till she had brought forth her firstborn son* (Matthew 1:24–25).

In addition to this, Terry also taught me that Jesus had brothers and sisters.

> *Then His brothers and His mother came, and standing outside they sent to Him, calling Him. And a multitude was sitting around Him; and they said to Him, "Look, Your mother and Your brothers are outside seeking You"* (Mark 3:31–32, NKJV).

> *Is this not the carpenter's son? Is not His mother called Mary? And His brothers James, Joses, Simon, and Judas? And, His sisters, are they not all with us?* (Matthew 13:55–56, NKJV).

These verses of Scripture were extremely important for me. After Terry had showed me these verses, I no longer saw Mary as a god or divine. I saw her as a person like you or me, created for God's own purpose. Mary was not to be worshipped but was to carry and give birth to the Christ whom we are to worship.

I was so excited to see Matthew 13:55–56 is nearly the same in the KJV as in the NKJV. I had thought I had to go to the NKJV to read of our Lord's brothers, which are clearly mentioned in the Bible. However, I can discover the same truth when reading the Scriptures in the King James Version. Only one word is different in the two versions: "And his brethren, James, and Joses, and Simon, and Judas? And his sisters, are they not all with us?" (Matthew 13:55–56). Clearly our Lord had brothers and sisters born after Him through His parents Joseph and Mary.

When I was first shown one of these verses of Scripture revealing that our Lord had brothers and sisters, I answered with my trained response: "Well, they are just speaking of 'brothers and sisters in Christ.'" I had been taught to give this explanation by my teachers, the Catholic nuns and priests. However, once I read these verses of Scripture, I believed Christ had siblings. After having had time to think about my answer to Terry, I began to realize it was impossible for Jesus to have had "brothers and sisters in Christ" at this point of time because our Lord had not yet offered Himself on the Cross and the church had not yet been established. In the context of Mark 3:31–32 and Matthew 13:55–56, the references clearly were speaking of the literal family members of Jesus.

> *Then one said to Him,* **"Look, Your mother and Your brothers are standing outside, seeking to speak with You."** *But He answered and said to the one who told Him, "Who is My mother and who are My brothers?" And He stretched out His hand toward His disciples and said, "Here are My mother and My brothers! "For whoever does the will of My Father in heaven is My brother and sister and mother"* (Matthew 12:47–50, NKJV).

Matthew 12:47–50 illustrates typical usage of the terms "brother" and "sister" in the Scriptures. Matthew 12:47 clearly refers to His literal family members, but Jesus went on in verses 48–50 to refer to His disciples as His "mother" and "brothers" because they were doing His will and pursuing His mission. In His usage here He was pointing forward to the mission of the future church and setting a precedent for believers who one day would use the terms "brother" and "sister" as terms of endearment to refer to fellow believers, members of the family of God.

Come Unto ME

Jesus ultimately extended usage of the terms "brother" and "sister" to refer to all believers—members of the body of Christ. This concept gives hope to all believers that they, like Mary, can be born again into Christ's kingdom and become members of the body of Jesus Christ. By being obedient to God's will, the Lord then will call us His brothers and sisters!

CHAPTER SIX
MARY NEEDED A SAVIOR

WHEN I had learned that Mary was the beautiful mother of four or six children, I realized she was human, like me. Like all humans, Mary needed a Savior too in order to be saved and go to Heaven. In fact, she was with the other believers who were awaiting the Promise in the upper room and who received the baptism of the Holy Ghost on the Day of Pentecost. She neither achieved Heaven on her own good deeds nor made it to Heaven by her identity as the mother of Jesus Christ. The Book of Acts records Mary's salvation along with the others who were born again at the inaugural beginning of the church. Lacking divinity, Mary could neither be my mediator nor my Savior.

When I saw that Mary needed a Savior, I knew since she needed one I needed a Savior too. It was difficult at first for me to realize Mary needed salvation because I had been taught she was without sin. However, the Scriptures reveal that all humankind are sinners without exception. I could not go against the Word of God for it is true. I now recognize that the Bible teaches everyone needs a Savior and Jesus is that Savior.

It is vital to back up what we believe through the Scriptures. After all, without the Bible how would we know that Jesus is the Christ or that Jesus would be born of a virgin? We find that answer in the prophecies of the Old Testament Scriptures. Further, the Lord Jesus even said in His own words: "Sanctify them through thy truth: thy word is truth" (John 17:17). This is how we know as Christians whether or not we are staying on track with the truth. However, my Catholic knowledge about Mary did not come from Scripture. We were not taught from the Word of God about Mary. Instead, we were taught about Mary by the Catholic nuns and priests from her so-called sightings. Most of what I had been taught about Mary in the Catholic Church was not backed up with Scripture. The Apostle Paul gave a solemn warning about how we handle the gospel and the Scriptures:

> *But though we, or an angel from heaven, preach any other gospel unto you than that which we have preached unto you, let him be accursed* (Galatians 1:8).

When I read these verses years ago about being accursed from God by listening to another gospel, I was frightened. I was frightened because I had been listening to false reports of these sightings claiming to be Mary. I did not want to be cursed by believing in these false reports so I was inspired to get my life right with God. I wanted to know I was abiding by only the truth of the Scriptures.

As hard as it was for me to believe, I had to accept that Mary was neither my savior nor without sin. This understanding was not "putting her down." The biblical meaning is clear. Mary was a good and godly woman, but I had learned she was neither a god nor divine. I learned she is not a source of salvation and that Mary herself needed redemption. She probably was not guilty of committing horrible sins, but she was a sinner who needed redemption. That she was able to be sensitive to hearing and obeying God seems to reveal her godly character and behavior, but that did not make her deity. She must have been seeking God because she found favor with Him, but she still needed to be redeemed.

The Bible is clear when it states all have sinned. Romans 3:12 proclaims, "They are all gone out of the way, they are together be-

Mary Needed a Savior

come unprofitable; there is none that doeth good, no, not one." Even though Mary was a godly woman, seeking the Lord and obeying God's will, she still was subject to the human plight of sin along with the rest of humankind.

Further, the Scriptures teach that by faith all can be cleansed from sin:

> *Even the righteousness of God which is by faith of Jesus Christ unto all and upon all them that believe: for there is no difference: For all have sinned, and come short of the glory of God; Being justified freely by his grace through the redemption that is in Christ Jesus: Whom God hath set forth to be a propitiation through faith in his blood, to declare his righteousness for the remission of sins that are past, through the forbearance of God; To declare, I say, at this time his righteousness: that he might be just, and the justifier of him which believeth in Jesus* (Romans 3:22-26).

The Catholic priests and nuns had taught us that the sins of mankind did not pass down to the Christ Child because of Mary's own sinless state due to her virginity. However, this interpretation of Mary is incorrect. The sins of mankind were passed down to the generations because of the fathers, not because of the sins of the mother. The Scriptures reveal that sin entered the human family through the sins of the fathers and was passed down through the generations through the fathers:

> *Keeping mercy for thousands, forgiving iniquity and transgression and sin, and that will by no means clear the guilty; visiting the iniquity of the fathers upon the children, and upon the children's children, unto the third and to the fourth generation* (Exodus 34:7).

Romans 5:12 mentions that sin entered the world by Adam, "Wherefore, as by one man sin entered into the world, and death by sin; and so death passed upon all men, for that all have sinned." Therefore, Christ is without sin not because of Mary, but because of Christ's sinless father, the Holy Ghost.

> Now the birth of Jesus Christ was on this wise: When as his mother Mary was espoused to Joseph, before they came together, she was found with child of the Holy Ghost (Matthew 1:18).

Christ Jesus did not have an earthly father to pass the sins of humankind down to Him. For this reason Jesus Christ was and is sinless. We worship Christ because of His deity, for He was conceived by the Holy Ghost. God Himself was manifested in that child. I Timothy 3:16 further explains the deity of Jesus:

> And without controversy great is the mystery of godliness: God was manifest in the flesh, justified in the Spirit, seen of angels, preached unto the Gentiles, believed on in the world, received up into glory.

The child Jesus was holy and sinless because God Himself was in Christ that He might redeem the world through Him. Consequently, the sins of mankind did not pass down to Him. Many Scriptures state that Jesus Christ knew no sin. I really had to reach a place of comprehending that Jesus is the only One without sin. Other Scriptures also express this truth. I Peter 2:21–22 further reveals His sinlessness:

> For even hereunto were ye called: because Christ also suffered for us, leaving us an example, that ye should follow his steps: Who did no sin, neither was guile found in his mouth.

Mary Needed a Savior

Jesus was sinless for He was the only lamb without blemish.

> *Forasmuch as ye know that ye were not redeemed with corruptible things, as silver and gold, from your vain conversation received by tradition from your fathers; but with the precious blood of Christ, as of a lamb without blemish and without spot: Who verily was foreordained before the foundation of the world, but was manifest in these last times for you. Who by him do believe in God, that raised him up from the dead, and gave him glory; that your faith and hope might be in God* (I Peter 1:18–21).

Jesus Christ offered Himself without spot, a righteous sacrifice offered through the eternal Spirit:

> *But Christ being come an high priest of good things to come, by a greater and more perfect tabernacle, not made with hands, that is to say, not of this building; Neither by the blood of goats and calves, but by his own blood he entered in once into the holy place, having obtained eternal redemption for us. For if the blood of bulls and of goats, and the ashes of an heifer sprinkling the unclean, sanctifieth to the purifying of the flesh; How much more shall the blood of Christ, who through the eternal Spirit offered himself without spot to God, purge your conscience from dead works to serve the living God? And for this cause he is the mediator of the new testament, that by means of death, for the redemption of the transgressions that were under the first testament, they which are called might receive the promise of eternal inheritance* (Hebrews 9:11–15).

Nowhere do the Scriptures include Mary as our savior or as a spotless lamb who would be sacrificed for our sins. Further, II Corinthians 5:17–21 declares that believers who are reconciled to God by Jesus' ministry of reconciliation become new creations, born again. He does not impute our trespasses unto us but makes us the righteousness of God in Jesus:

> *Therefore, if any man be in Christ, he is a new creature: old things are passed away; behold, all things are become new. And all things are of God, who hath reconciled us to himself by Jesus Christ, and hath given to us the ministry of reconciliation; To wit, that God was in Christ, reconciling the world unto himself, not imputing their trespasses unto them; and hath committed unto us the word of reconciliation. Now then we are ambassadors for Christ, as though God did beseech you by us: we pray you in Christ's stead, be ye reconciled to God. For he hath made him to be sin for us, who knew no sin; that we might be made the righteousness of God in him.*

God had changed my focus; now I was no longer looking to Mary to redeem me from my sins, but to Jesus as my Savior. The Old Testament confirms there is only one savior: "I, even I, am the LORD; and beside me there is no savior" (Isaiah 43:11). Our Lord Jesus is that only Savior, and I learned Mary had not given me this chance of salvation. God came to us through Jesus Christ, the Son of God, a gift of redemption to all humankind.

These and other verses of Scripture throughout the Bible revealed to me that there is no salvation through Mary, nor will there ever be. Mary needed a Savior to make it to Heaven just as we do. Even Mary understood her need of salvation and she even voiced her need of a savior. In her conversation with Elizabeth, Mary said, "My soul doth magnify the Lord, And my spirit hath rejoiced in God my Savior" (Luke 1:46–47). Mary knew she needed a savior too!

Mary Needed a Savior

In Luke 1:45, Elizabeth had stated to Mary, "And blessed is she that believed: for there shall be a performance of those things which were told her from the Lord." After reading this, I asked myself, *What performance? Was the Savior of the world coming because Mary was without sin?* No, not at all. Rather, Mary believed what the angel had spoken to her. God carried out His words spoken through the angel to Mary because she believed, not because she was without sin. Mary didn't just believe she would be expecting but that she would be expecting "the Son of the Highest," who would also become her Savior. Look again at what the angel of the Lord had spoken to Mary:

And the angel said unto her, Fear not, Mary: for thou hast found favour with God. And, behold, thou shalt conceive in thy womb, and bring forth a son, and shalt call his name JESUS. He shall be great, and shall be called the Son of the Highest: and the Lord God shall give unto him the throne of his father David: And he shall reign over the house of Jacob for ever; and of his kingdom there shall be no end (Luke 1:30–33). *And she shall bring forth a son, and thou shalt call his name Jesus: for he shall save his people from their sins. Now all this was done, that it might be fulfilled which was spoken of the Lord by the prophet, saying, Behold, a virgin shall be with child, and shall bring forth a son, and they shall call his name Emmanuel, which being interpreted is, God with us* (Matthew 1:21–23).

After recognizing what the Scriptures were teaching me about the birth of Jesus Christ, I sensed the Lord bringing to my Catholic-trained mind the correct understanding of the Scriptures regarding the virgin birth. My new understanding of truth and my new focus on God was similar to the focus Mary had on God. She had a revelation of who God was and knew she needed a Savior, which she had readily acknowledged to Elizabeth.

Further, the Book of Acts relates that Mary was present at Pentecost to obtain her salvation. Mary needed to receive the baptism of the Holy Ghost to make it to Heaven:

> *And when they were come in, they went up into an upper room, where abode both Peter, and James, and John, and Andrew, Philip, and Thomas, Bartholomew, and Matthew, James the son of Alphaeus, and Simon Zelotes, and Judas the brother of James. These all continued with one accord in prayer and supplication, with the women, and Mary the mother of Jesus, and with his brethren* (Acts 1:13–14).

Mary and her other children were there at Pentecost. She did not make it to Heaven on her own merit as I had been taught. Therefore, since Mary needed a savior, we all need a Savior.

At this point in my life I knew I had repented of my sins and received the Holy Spirit. However, I did not know the full plan of salvation. I had received only two parts of God's plan of salvation, and I sensed something still was missing. I did not know what it was at the time, but I had to find out.

Not wanting to remain in the Catholic charismatic movement, I no longer desired to practice worshiping Mary. Another person in the Catholic charismatic movement told me she also felt the Holy Ghost moving on her not to worship Mary any longer. I knew from what I had read about Mary being at Pentecost that she had found salvation and I wanted this too. Some of the women in the Catholic charismatic movement were also sharing with me they felt the Holy Ghost instructing them to appear more feminine by allowing their hair to grow and by wearing dresses. We didn't at that time understand the teachings of Scripture regarding these biblical truths, but still the Holy Ghost was trying to teach us and lead us. I wasn't sure of what to do next, but I understood I had to leave the Catholic Church.

CHAPTER SEVEN
BREAKING AWAY
FROM THE CATHOLIC CHURCH

SIX more months had gone by from the time when I had received the Holy Ghost and Terry had begun teaching me. At this point, it had been about a year since I first received the Holy Spirit and I felt as if the Spirit was directing me to leave the Catholic Church. By now, I had seen too much truth to remain a Catholic. During this time I experienced many heartaches and walked through many conflicts. I did not make my decision to leave the Catholic Church overnight, and I received many calls from friends and relatives in the church and the larger Catholic Charismatic movement who were trying to convince me to stay.

My brother, Will, who had invited me to the Catholic Charismatic movement, had the strongest influence with me. Will told me he was sorry I had ever received the baptism of the Holy Ghost. Steadfast, I responded that I was not sorry. The Holy Ghost was the best thing that had ever happened to me. I would not be alive were it not for the Holy Ghost. I kept secret the physical abuse I had suffered through that year and the times the Lord had kept me alive. I did not tell him how I'd been thrown against walls, dragged by my ankles up flights of stairs just because I wanted to go to the prayer meetings. Through all this, however, I never missed a time of scheduled prayer. I was there every Wednesday night. Nothing was going to stop me from attending; the Lord was all I had. He was everything to me. The Lord had given me life in more ways than one. I remained sweet, but firm with my brother, just as Terry had been with me.

When Will would call, I began to share with him the things the Lord had showed me. I began telling Will that I was reading my Bible. Then my brother began inviting me to have a Bible study with his group, which was being led by a Catholic priest. I sensed from the Holy Ghost that a play was being made for my soul. I responded to my brother, "Why would I want a priest who does not have the baptism of the Holy Ghost explain to me what the Scriptures mean when I have the Spirit living inside of me? Who could better explain the Scriptures to me?" I thought I would much rather listen to the Holy Ghost. This way I could know for certain that what I was learning was true since it was coming from God Himself. With my whole heart, I believed the Holy Ghost living inside of me could teach me the meaning of the Scriptures. The week prior to this conversation with my brother the Holy Ghost had shown me this Scripture in Hebrews:

> *For this is the covenant that I will make with the house of Israel after those days, says the Lord: I will put My laws in their mind and write them on their hearts; and I will be their God, and they shall be My people. None of them shall teach his neighbor, and none his brother, saying, 'Know the Lord,' for all shall know Me, from the least of them to the greatest of them* (Hebrews 8:10–11, NKJV).

Truly, I believed I was one of the "least" of these mentioned by the writer of Hebrews. Also, with the Holy Ghost living inside my heart, I knew God Himself could correct me and teach me. God could teach me more about Himself and His truths than a priest could teach me. After all, the Holy Spirit was already doing this. At this point in my life, I wanted more than anything to continue living for God. It was the desire of my heart for God to continue correcting me and to continue teaching me. I wanted to know the Lord more, and more.

Breaking Away from the Catholic Church

Still, the conversations with my brother continued. I tried to reason with him, but my brother refused to listen. Instead, he went back to the Catholic priest and told him I was continuing to read my Bible at home. Yes, my brother "told on me" to the priest; so the pressures increased. They told me the Catholic Church did not allow me to read my Bible at home, but that I was only allowed to read my Bible in the presence of a Catholic priest. As my brother continued to pressure me, I continued to witness to my brother. During these times the Holy Ghost reminded me of Scriptures that I was able to quote to my brother, but these calls were quickly coming to an end. Finally, my brother stated that he could no longer speak to me. He suggested I could no longer understand the Catholic ways and practices because I was no longer willing to obey the Catholic priests and doctrines. I tried to speak to my brother about the importance of the words of the Bible, but he simply stated, "We have Mary now, and we no longer need the Bible." With these sad words we parted company, but I continue to pray for him. I have shed many tears and offered many prayers for my brother's salvation.

Our parting was not without heartache. This was my closest brother. As a child, when my older brothers would beat up on me and even leave me unconscious, this brother would step in to defend me and even take the beatings for me. It was difficult for me to watch his and my relationship crumble, but I knew I was not alone, and I still am confident of Christ's companionship to this day. Many believers have to choose between serving God and meeting the demands of their families. However, our relationship with the Almighty far outweighs any earthly relationships. While reading my Bible I came across a verse of Scripture that addressed the personal turmoil I was experiencing: "He that loveth father or mother more than me is not worthy of me: and he that loveth son or daughter more than me is not worthy of me" (Matthew 10:37).

Our decisions determine our eternity. I want to be saved and make it to Heaven, worship at Christ's feet, and express my love for Him.

I had made my decision and with the help of the Lord I was breaking free. However, more turbulence was on the horizon. My brother notified my dad of what was going on between us, and my dad began to call me. "Daughter," he'd say, "We will have you taken off of every will if you break free from the Catholic Church." I told him, "Dad, you will have to do what you feel you need to do, but I'm not changing my mind." Then he increased the pressure even more. He said, "I'll make sure to have you taken off of your godfather's will." My godfather was a multi-millionaire. When he threatened this action, I thought, *What good did his millions do for him. His son was locked up in a padded cell for trying to pull a gun on his mother and sister at a young age.* My godfather flew his son away in a private Lear jet, endeavoring to escape their troubles. When his son was eighteen, they flew him back home and gave him a new car and money, thinking it would resolve his inner problems. To their surprise their son walked away from it all to live on the streets of Valetta Beach—living as a bum, a drug addict, and in jail every week. Again, I thought, *What did his millions do for him? They had no home life.*

I sweetly and respectfully told my dad, "Dad, you will have to do what you have to do." He would have to decide for himself what actions he would take because my mind was made up. I was living for God. Finally he said, "Daughter, we will disown you." The words stung. I told him, "Dad, I'm not giving up the Holy Ghost. It is your decision." My salvation was not up for sale—not at any cost. My family didn't speak to me and had nothing to do with me for a while, although I cannot recall how long it continued. However, God is so good and faithful. Despite my decision to live for God, after some time they began to speak to me again.

Breaking Away from the Catholic Church

In time, my godfather passed away. Shortly after his passing, my dad had my godmother to call me. I do not know what the role of a godparent is in other Catholic families, but I know how it was in my family. I was not taught this in the Catholic private school I attended as a child, but my parents taught me that a godparent was someone who had taken a Catholic vow to make sure their godchild remained Catholic—no matter what. The call came, and it was not good.

These were trying times, but I'm sharing my situation to help encourage other Catholics who may be experiencing or about to experience similar trials. God is greater than any trial. I no longer had a godfather, but I had Someone far greater. I had gained a heavenly Father.

Other Catholics close to me called to say, "Once a Catholic, always a Catholic." That statement is not true. With a made-up mind, I left the Catholic Church and began searching for the moving of the Lord's Spirit in many other churches. Even though I had felt the presence of the Holy Ghost in some of these churches, in my heart I felt as if something was missing. A passage of Scripture kept coming to me:

> Not every one that saith unto me, Lord, Lord, shall enter into the kingdom of heaven; but he that doeth the will of my Father which is in heaven. Many will say to me in that day, Lord, Lord, have we not prophesied in thy name? and in thy name have cast out devils? and in thy name done many wonderful works? And then will I profess unto them, I never knew you: depart from me, ye that work iniquity. Therefore whosoever heareth these sayings of mine, and doeth them, I will liken him unto a wise man, which built his house upon a rock: And the rain descended, and the floods came, and the winds blew, and beat upon that house; and it fell not: for it was founded upon a rock (Matthew 7:21–25).

Come Unto ME

I continued searching for what God was trying to teach me from my Bible. The search took me through many more visits to various churches and discussions about the Scriptures with many people. During this time I endeavored to grow closer to Christ.

The following two chapters detail some of the biblical discoveries I made during my search as I was transitioning from Catholicism and following my departure.

CHAPTER EIGHT
THE OLD AND NEW TESTAMENT TABERNACLES

IN the first year after breaking away from the Catholic Church, the Lord began to show me a new area of interest. My concerns began while reading Hebrews 8:5, where it states: "who serve the copy and shadow of heavenly things, as Moses was divinely instructed when he was about to make the tabernacle" (NKJV). After reading this, I started to wonder if there were many similarities and differences in the New and Old Testaments. I also wanted to know if the Old Testament was a "shadow" so to speak of the New Testament in which we are now living. In addition to all of this, I wanted to know what was meant by the word "tabernacle."

Consider, for instance, the Lord's crucifixion in the New Testament. There is one event of the Crucifixion in particular that captures my attention. After our Lord Jesus died on the cross, the veil (curtain) in the Hebrew Temple was supernaturally torn in two, from the top to the bottom. I wondered what could be so significant about the veil being torn. The account of the tearing of the veil is recorded in three of the Gospels. The Book of Matthew describes the event:

> *Jesus, when he had cried again with a loud voice, yielded up the ghost. And, behold, the veil of the temple was rent in twain from the top to the bottom; and the earth did quake, and the rocks rent* (Matthew 27:50–51).

The tearing of the veil made me think about the Catholic altar, which also has a golden tabernacle with small curtains divided in the front. The thought of the two tabernacles made me curious, so I began to look up the word tabernacle in the New Testament.

> *In that he saith, A new covenant, he hath made the first old. Now that which decayeth and waxeth old is ready to vanish away. Then verily the first covenant had also ordinances of divine service, and a worldly sanctuary. For there was a tabernacle made; the first, wherein was the candlestick, and the table, and the shewbread; which is called the sanctuary. And after the second veil, the tabernacle which is called the Holiest of all; Which had the golden censer, and the ark of the covenant overlaid round about with gold, wherein was the golden pot that had manna, and Aaron's rod that budded, and the tables of the covenant; And over it the cherubims of glory shadowing the mercyseat; of which we cannot now speak particularly* (Hebrews 8:13–9:5).

The time of Jesus' death on the cross is the moment the New Testament began, and the Old Testament Tabernacle became obsolete. This truth we know, but there was more symbolism involved than only that transition from one covenant to another. The veiled curtain was in front of the Holy of Holies where the presence of God dwelt symbolically in the time of the Old Testament. I learned when the veil of the Temple was torn, it symbolized the truth that access to God's Spirit was no longer confined to only the Holy of Holies, but that all mankind could access His presence, and they no longer had to enter the Temple's Holy of Holies. Since the Day of Pentecost, we now know God's Spirit can dwell in our hearts through the Baptism of the Holy Ghost, and our bodies have united as the body of Christ to become the new tabernacle. The Old Testament symbols were the

The Old and New Testament Tabernacles

shadow of things that were to come in the New Testament.

Instead, as a former Catholic, we were incorrectly considering the Old Testament in a concrete sense, rather than as types and shadows of a spiritual experience to come. Being a Catholic, certain words in the above verses of Scripture stood out from others in the passage: *obsolete, veil, tabernacle, gold,* and *manna.* These words stood out to me because we had on our Catholic altar a golden tabernacle with a veil in front of the manna, which we called the "host." With curiosity, I then began to read more in the Old Testament about the Tabernacle.

> *And it came to pass in the first month in the second year, on the first day of the month, that the tabernacle was reared up. And Moses reared up the tabernacle, and fastened his sockets, and set up the boards thereof, and put in the bars thereof, and reared up his pillars. And he spread abroad the tent over the tabernacle, and put the covering of the tent above upon it; as the Lord commanded Moses.*
>
> *And he took and put the testimony into the ark, and set the staves on the ark, and put the mercy seat above upon the ark: And he brought the ark into the tabernacle, and set up the vail of the covering, and covered the ark of the testimony; as the Lord commanded Moses.*
>
> *And he put the table in the tent of the congregation, upon the side of the tabernacle northward, without the vail. And he set the bread in order upon it before the Lord; as the Lord had commanded Moses.*
>
> *And he put the candlestick in the tent of the congregation, over against the table, on the side of the tabernacle southward. And he lighted the lamps before the Lord; as the Lord commanded Moses.*

> *And he put the golden altar in the tent of the congregation before the vail: And he burnt sweet incense thereon; as the Lord commanded Moses.*
>
> *And he set up the hanging at the door of the tabernacle. And he put the altar of burnt offering by the door of the tabernacle of the tent of the congregation, and offered upon it the burnt offering and the meat offering; as the Lord commanded Moses.*
>
> *And he set the laver between the tent of the congregation and the altar, and put water there, to wash withal. And Moses and Aaron and his sons washed their hands and their feet thereat: When they went into the tent of the congregation, and when they came near unto the altar, they washed; as the Lord commanded Moses* (Exodus 40:18–32).

When I read Exodus 40, I thought to myself: *At the Catholic mass, we have a golden tabernacle behind a veil, and our priests wash their hands before and after reaching into the tabernacle.* The priests even washed their hands before and after touching the holy items on our Catholic altar. I thought it unusual to find similarities between our Catholic services, and the Old Testament services. I thought again of our Lord dying on the cross, and the veil of the Temple tearing in two. I thought, *Why have we as Catholics then put up a new golden tabernacle made with hands, and sewn on a new curtain in front of it?"* Then I realized, *I don't want to live in another recreated Old Testament. I want to live in the New Testament with the new covenant provided by Christ Himself.* I read in the Bible that the Old Tabernacle is obsolete and that it has already passed away. (See Hebrews 8–9.) Wanting to find out more, I continued reading in the Old Testament.

The Old and New Testament Tabernacles

I discovered additional similarities that greatly paralleled our Catholic services. Our Catholic priests wore special robes for the services reminiscent of the Old Testament priests who wore special robes for their services. Exodus 39 gives us information concerning the priestly garments.

> *Of the blue and purple and scarlet thread they made garments of ministry, for ministering in the holy place and made the holy garments for Aaron, as the* LORD *had commanded Moses. He made the ephod of gold and blue and purple and scarlet thread, and of fine linen thread. And they beat the gold into thin sheets and cut it into threads, to work it in with the blue and purple and scarlet and fine linen thread, into artistic designs. They made shoulder straps for it to couple it together; it was coupled together at its two edges. And the intricately woven band of his ephod that was on it was of the same workmanship, woven of gold and blue and purple and scarlet thread, and fine linen thread, as the* LORD *had commanded Moses* (Exodus 39:1–5, NKJV).

Exodus 39:41 (NKJV) clarifies further that Aaron and the priests had to wear special garments: "And the garments of ministry, to minister in the holy place: the holy garments for Aaron the priest, and his sons' garments, to minister as priests." The Catholic priests wore special garments for the services. Some garments in the Catholic services were even more elaborate for holy days. Further, the Catholic priests' garments were also considered to be holy just as the Jewish priests' garments were considered holy unto the Lord. If someone accidentally touched a priest's sleeve while shaking his hand, it was considered a sin. One would then need to visit a confessional to repent of the sin to the priest. At that time an atonement of specific prayers was assigned to the guilty individual to recite in order to receive forgiveness.

The Jewish people also went to the Jewish priests to confess and offer atonement for their sins. As a Catholic, I too went to a priest during confession and later offered up an atonement of certain prayers for forgiveness of certain sins. However, the New Testament says, "This is the covenant that I will make with them after those days, saith the Lord, I will put my laws into their hearts, and in their minds will I write them; And their sins and iniquities will I remember no more. Now where remission of these is, there is no more offering for sin" (Hebrews 10:16–18).

When I read Hebrews 10:16–18, I knew I no longer needed to go to a human priest for confession and to repeat certain prayers for forgiveness of sins. Instead, I could go to my High Priest, the Lord of lords, which is Jesus Christ, and ask Him for forgiveness in privacy. He would be just to forgive me and to forget my transgressions. He required no memorized official prayer that was to be recited so I could be forgiven. I recognized that forgiveness of sins needed to be based on God's Word, not on human traditions. What freedom I felt!

I John 1:9 revealed to me that "If we confess our sins, he is faithful and just to forgive us our sins, and to cleanse us from all unrighteousness." John restated that Jesus was my confessor. We are to confess our sins to Jesus only.

> *Then said Jesus to those Jews which believed on him, If ye continue in my word, then are ye my disciples indeed; and ye shall know the truth, and the truth shall make you free* (John 8:31–32).

I was feeling the freedom of being able to confess to the Lord from my heart. However, lest my motives be unclear, I am in no way

The Old and New Testament Tabernacles

denigrating the people of my former practices. Hosea 4:6 speaks of what happens to people when there is a lack of knowledge: "My people are destroyed for lack of knowledge." I don't want to be destroyed and I do not want my own people to be destroyed for lack of knowledge. My desire was to be certain of my salvation and of making it to Heaven to be with our Lord. And I want the same thing for all Catholics. As Catholics, we were taught if the priests were wrong in what they taught us "they would automatically go to hell, but that we would still make it to Heaven out of sheer ignorance."

How could I be sure of this? I couldn't. Then I read two verses of Scripture that address individual responsibility for salvation. In Romans 14:12, I read, "So then every one of us shall give account of himself to God." In similar fashion, Philippians 2:12 states, "Wherefore, my beloved, as ye have always obeyed, not as in my presence only, but now much more in my absence, work out your own salvation with fear and trembling." We cannot rely on ignorance to save us! We must read and study God's Word for ourselves and obey the Scriptures.

These verses of Scripture were different from anything I had been taught while growing up. These instructions became one of my goals for finding this salvation of which the Lord had spoken. Unquestionably, it would be disastrous to think one was "certain" of going to Heaven only to be turned away at the pearly gates. Salvation would be far too late at that point, which Scripture reveals.

> *"Not everyone who says to me, 'Lord, Lord,' shall enter the kingdom of heaven, but he who does the will of My Father in heaven. Many will say to Me in that day, 'Lord, Lord, have we not prophesied in Your name, cast out demons in Your name, and done many wonders in Your name?' And then I will declare to them, 'I never knew you;*

depart from Me, you who practice lawlessness!' (Matthew 7:21–23, NKJV).

After reading these Scripture passages as well as other verses of Scripture from the Old Testament, I thought, *I no longer want to live in the Old Testament, but I want to live in the New Testament.* Therefore, I journeyed again to the New Testament Scriptures to seek out more words that had to do with "tabernacle" and "priest." What I was to find was most wonderful:

> *Now of the things which we have spoken this is the sum: we have such an high priest, who is set on the right hand of the throne of the Majesty in the heavens; A minister of the sanctuary, and of the true tabernacle, which the Lord pitched, and not man. . . . In that he saith, A new covenant, he hath made the first old. Now that which decayeth and waxeth old is ready to vanish away* (Hebrews 8:1–2, 13). (See the entire chapter of Hebrews 8; also, compare with NKJV.)

Hebrews 9 also speaks of these covenants. It is important to note that all individuals have an appointment with death, after which is the judgment (Hebrews 9:27). This reveals that there is no purgatory, for judgment follows our death!

> *For Christ is not entered into the holy places made with hands, which are the figures of the true; but into heaven itself, now to appear in the presence of God for us: Nor yet that he should offer himself often, as the high priest entereth into the holy place every year with blood of others; For then must he often have suffered since the foundation of the world: but now once in the end of the world hath he appeared to put away sin by the sacrifice of*

The Old and New Testament Tabernacles

himself. And as it is appointed unto men once to die, but after this the judgment:

(Please notice from this bolded statement "but after this the judgment" — there is no purgatory.)

So Christ was once offered to bear the sins of many; and unto them that look for him shall he appear the second time without sin unto salvation (Hebrews 9:24–28). (See the entire chapter of Hebrews 9 for further comparisons with the Old Testament Tabernacle and priestly services. Also, compare with Hebrews 9, NKJV.)

Again, I emphasize, there is **no purgatory**! Since there is no purgatory, we have only this short, human life in which we may secure our salvation; there will not be another opportunity beyond this life. Since "Christ has not entered the holy places made with hands which are copies of the true" (Hebrews 9:24), then what is the new holy place not made with human hands? The Apostle Peter answered this question for us: "Yea, I think it meet, as long as I am in this tabernacle, to stir you up by putting you in remembrance; Knowing that shortly I must put off this my tabernacle, even as our Lord Jesus Christ hath shewed me. Moreover I will endeavor that ye may be able after my decease to have these things always in remembrance" (II Peter 1:13–15).

Peter clearly was writing about his approaching execution and referencing his body as his tabernacle. Also, Paul wrote in I Corinthians 3:16 that our bodies are temples of the Spirit of God: "Know ye not that ye are the temple of God, and that the Spirit of God dwelleth in you?"

From the Scriptures we know our bodies have become the new tabernacle/temple of God when we receive the Holy Spirit of God living in us. How does one know if he or she has received the Spirit of God? The Book of Acts gives the answer:

> *And when the day of Pentecost was fully come, they were all with one accord in one place. And suddenly there came a sound from heaven as of a rushing mighty wind, and it filled all the house where they were sitting. And there appeared unto them cloven tongues like as of fire, and it sat upon each of them. And they were all filled with the Holy Ghost, and began to speak with other tongues, as the Spirit gave them utterance* (Acts 2:1–4).

These truths summon new questions. Is the Day of Pentecost only for the time of the Apostles to bring about the New Testament as we had been taught as Catholics? Or, is the Day of Pentecost for all the church age until Jesus Christ returns for His people? Apostle Peter answered these questions, which we address in the next chapter.

CHAPTER NINE
THE APOSTLE PETER AND WATER BAPTISM

NOT all Catholics are followers of Mary, but instead they profess to be followers of the Apostle Peter, for many Catholics believe Peter was the first pope. They also believe Peter started the first Catholic Church. This they assume because of a misinterpretation from Peter's confession recorded in the Book of Matthew.

He saith unto them, But whom say ye that I am? And Simon Peter answered and said, Thou art the Christ, the Son of the living God. And Jesus answered and said unto him, Blessed art thou, Simon Barjona: for flesh and blood hath not revealed it unto thee, but my Father which is in heaven. And I say also unto thee, That thou art Peter, and upon this rock I will build my church; and the gates of hell shall not prevail against it. And I will give unto thee the keys of the kingdom of heaven: and whatsoever thou shalt bind on earth shall be bound in heaven: and whatsoever thou shalt loose on earth shall be loosed in heaven (Matthew 16:15–19).

> *The Lord revealed He was giving Peter the foundational truths concerning His church. However, Catholics generally misunderstand this exchange between Jesus and Peter and they place undue emphasis on the phrase, "Thou art Peter, and upon this rock I will build my church" (Matthew 16:18).*

The nuns and priests taught us this means Peter was the rock and he built the Catholic Church. The misinterpretation of this verse of Scripture results from the failure to focus on Peter's answer to the question Jesus asked him. Christ asked His apostles, "But whom say ye that I am?" Peter answered, **"Thou art the Christ, the Son of the living God"** (Matthew 16:15–16). Peter had a revelation of who Christ was. In truth, Jesus is the Rock and the foundation upon which the New Testament Church was to be built: **"upon this rock I will build my church."** Jesus is the Rock as seen in I Corinthians 10:4: "And did all drink the same spiritual drink: for they drank of that spiritual Rock that followed them: and that Rock was Christ."

It is true that the Greek form of Peter's name means "a piece of rock," however, the word for Peter's name is different from the word used to describe Jesus Christ as the foundation of the church, which means "a mass of rock." What is the difference between a "small piece of stone" and a "huge foundational rock?" The difference has to do with size and ability to serve as a foundation, supporting a great structure that is built thereon. A small stone is hard and strong, but it alone could never serve as a foundation. A huge mass of rock, however, is hard, strong, and large, thereby having the ability to support whatever structure is built upon it.

The contrasting use of these different Greek words in the conversation between Jesus and Peter illuminates the different roles of Peter and Christ within the church. Peter played an important role in the church, but he is not the foundation. Jesus Christ, on the other hand, is the very foundation upon which the entire structure of the church is built. When compared to the role of Christ, Peter's role was only a small role. *Strong's Greek/English Concordance* provides the following definitions of the two different words:

> "*Petros,*" Peter's name ("Thou art Peter," Matthew 16:18): "*Petros;* apparently a primary word; a (piece of) rock (larger than 3037); as a name, Petrus, an apostle:— Peter, rock."

The Apostle Peter and Water Baptism

"*Petra*," foundation "rock" of the church ("upon this 'rock' I will build my church," Matthew 16:18): "*Petra*;. . . a (mass of) rock (literally or figuratively):— rock. . . . a rock, cliff or ledge, a projecting rock, crag, rocky ground, a rock, a large stone."

"*Petra*," Christ the Foundation ("that Rock was Christ, I Corinthians 10:4): "*Petra*" . . . . (same definition as above).

A close examination of the word usage in the original Greek language of these two passages reveals the contrasting roles of Peter and Jesus with regard to Christ's church. Peter's role in establishing the beginning of the church was important, but his role ended and he was not the foundation; Peter's confession of the divine identity of Jesus Christ (Matthew 16:16) was a significant piece of the foundation of the church, but Peter himself was not that foundation. Jesus Christ, on the other hand, is the foundation of the church and His role in His church is vital and without end.

The Bible does not record Peter ever being called the first pope. Neither could I find in the Bible where Peter preached in Rome. Instead, I found Peter preaching to the Jews in Jerusalem and Paul leaving Israel to preach to the Gentiles. Paul travelled throughout various countries such as Macedonia, Greece, and Rome preaching the message of the New Testament salvation to the Gentiles. The Book of Acts records Paul's missions to multiple countries. Further, I also discovered that Peter's primary mission was to the Jews:

> *But contrariwise, when they saw that the gospel of the uncircumcision was committed unto me, as the gospel of the circumcision was unto Peter; (For he that wrought effectually in Peter to the apostleship of the circumcision,*

the same was mighty in me toward the Gentiles:) (Galatians 2:7–8).

In reading my Bible, I noticed the early churches were called Christian churches and the early believers were called Christians. This idea was something to explore. With this in mind, I began to search the Bible for any Scriptures about what the early churches were called, and then discovered Acts 11:26:

And when he had found him, he brought him unto Antioch. And it came to pass, that a whole year they assembled themselves with the church, and taught much people. And the disciples were called Christians first in Antioch."

This Scripture showed me the early churches were not called Catholic churches. Instead, they were called Christian churches in Jerusalem and the surrounding countries. In addition, I came to grips with the fact the Holy Bible is the earliest recorded history of the early church, not Catholic encyclopedias. First and foremost, we as Christians must choose to believe the Bible!

Wanting to find a church preaching the full truth of salvation, I began checking out various churches. In one of these churches I overheard a conversation the pastor and elders were having that has stayed with me all of these years. They wondered what it would be like to step back into time. They wanted to hear the preaching and to hear the plan of salvation preached by the early apostles before 2,000 years of religion had time to influence people and cause changes to occur. They longed to hear what was absolutely necessary to make it to Heaven, and they wondered if they even had the plan of salvation. In their conversation they asked each other, "What did the early apostles preach?" This had my full attention. I left their group thinking, *If they don't know if they have the plan of salvation, what am*

I doing here? Wanting to find this plan of salvation and the preaching of the early apostles, I continued searching.

I also had another question that was unanswered. When I had attended the very first Christian prayer group where I worked with Terry, the Christians said something that had also stuck with me. When they prayed, they often "pled the blood of Jesus." I wanted to know what it meant to be covered by the blood of Jesus. I would ask people, "What does it mean to be covered with the blood?" They would say, "You know, the blood that was shed from the cross." Somehow this answer did not fully satisfy my curiosity.

Moreover, I felt there should be an experience to go along with understanding what it meant to be covered with the blood of Jesus. Since there was a difference between hearing about the baptism of the Holy Ghost and experiencing the baptism of the Holy Ghost, then there must also be a difference between knowing about the blood of Jesus and having experienced the covering of the blood.

Further, a Scripture kept coming to me from the Book of Revelation: "And they overcame him [meaning Satan] by the blood of the Lamb, and by the word of their testimony; and they loved not their lives unto the death" (Revelation 12:11). I had three things in mind as I continued my search for a Bible-believing, proclaiming church:

1. I desired the presence of the Holy Ghost;

2. I desired to understand about the blood; and

3. I desired the preaching of the apostles' doctrine.

I continued my search, going from church to church, seeking answers for these three key objectives in mind.

Come Unto ME

I did not immediately receive the answer to my search. After ten long years of searching churches, the Lord led me to an Apostolic Church where I could hear the preaching of the Apostles' doctrine—preaching that aligned with that of the Apostle Peter. To my delightful amazement, the first sermons I heard were preached directly from the Book of Acts. This book of the Bible is where the first sermons of the Apostles were recorded. I had read the Book of Acts possibly three times, but I had never noticed the Apostle Peter's first sermon from Acts 2. Not only was this Peter's first message, it is also the first sermon of the Apostles in the New Testament church.

Catholics thought Peter was the first Catholic Pope. Instead, my pastor taught me Peter was Pentecost's first preacher. It was revealed to me in his preaching that Peter stated clearly in his sermon what is essential for salvation. The Apostle Peter never preached seven sacraments to be saved. Instead, we discover the Apostle Peter preached three fundamental elements to the plan of salvation, following the Jews' recognition of Jesus as the Christ.

> *But Peter, standing up with the eleven, lifted up his voice, and said unto them, Ye men of Judea, and all ye that dwell at Jerusalem, be this known unto you, and hearken to my words: For these are not drunken, as ye suppose, seeing it is but the third hour of the day. But this is that which was spoken by the prophet Joel; And it shall come to pass in the last days, saith God, I will pour out of my Spirit upon all flesh: and your sons and your daughters shall prophesy, and your young men shall see visions, and your old men shall dream dreams: And on my servants and on my handmaidens I will pour out in those days of my Spirit; and they shall prophesy. . . . Therefore let all the house of Israel know assuredly, that God hath made that same Jesus, whom ye have crucified, both Lord and*

The Apostle Peter and Water Baptism

Christ. Now when they heard this, they were pricked in their heart, and said unto Peter and to the rest of the apostles, Men and brethren, what shall we do? Then Peter said unto them, **Repent, and be baptized every one of you in the name of Jesus Christ for the remission of sins, and ye shall receive the gift of the Holy Ghost. For the promise is unto you and to your children, and to all that are afar off, even as many as the Lord our God shall call** (Acts 2:14–39). *(For the full text of Peter's sermon, see the entire chapter.)*

Peter preached Christ's identity and willing sacrifice for the sins of all mankind. He further preached of their rejection of Him, His consequent crucifixion, and His victorious resurrection from the grave. With conviction and faith in Jesus Christ, they implored Peter to tell them what they should do to be saved. Peter preached they were to: 1. repent, 2. be baptized in water in the name of Jesus Christ for the remission of sins, and 3. be filled with the Holy Ghost.

As the pastor preached this message of Peter from nearly two millennia prior, it rang clear to me this message and experience were what I had been looking for! All the years of seeking had finally paid off. God had been faithful and brought the answer I had been looking for after all those years of searching, and I wanted it. I had first repented of my sins years before in the privacy of my bedroom, and daily since that time. I also had received the baptism of the Holy Spirit. However, the experience of water baptism had been missing, and this was the answer to my long years of searching. I needed water baptism in Jesus' name for the remission of my sins. Somehow, deep inside I knew I was incomplete and wanted my rebirth to be complete.

Prior to this revelation I had wondered if I needed to be water baptized. However, I had been water baptized as a baby. It was explained to me that I was too young as a baby to understand what was being done to me when I was water baptized in the Catholic Church. A baby has not committed any sins yet for which he or she would need to repent and for which he or she needed forgiveness. Further, a baby cannot repent.

It also is important to understand the meaning of baptism. In Acts 2:38, the word "baptized" is translated from the Greek word *baptizo*, which *Strong's Concordance* defines as "to immerse, submerge; to make whelmed (i. e. fully wet); used only (in the New Testament) of ceremonial ablution, especially (technically) of the ordinance of Christian baptism:—Baptist, baptize, wash. . . . to dip repeatedly, to immerse, to submerge (of vessels sunk) to cleanse by dipping or submerging, to wash, to make clean with water, to wash one's self, bathe to overwhelm."

Clearly, the word in the original text of the Scriptures refers to "dipping," "submerging," or "plunging" into the water, not to sprinkling, which is the mode used for infant baptism. Sprinkling an infant with water is not really water baptism at all. That is the reason Peter preached for believers to repent, be baptized in water in the name of Jesus Christ for the remission of sins, and receive the Holy Ghost. Repentance and water baptism go together, which is not something an infant can understand or experience.

However, I still needed a full understanding. The couple who had invited me to church, Reverend and Sister Johnstone, came to my home to give me a Bible study on water baptism. First, they started off with a prayer, asking the Lord to lead them. Then they both showed me Acts 2:38 on water baptism and the plan of salvation our Lord had taught His disciples:

The Apostle Peter and Water Baptism

> *Then Peter said unto them, Repent, and be baptized every one of you in the name of Jesus Christ for the remission of sins, and ye shall receive the gift of the Holy Ghost.*

Sister Johnstone and her husband then led me to Matthew 28:19:

> *Go ye therefore, and teach all nations, baptizing them in the **name** of the Father, and of the Son, and of the Holy Ghost.*

Then Brother Johnstone asked me a question that opened my eyes. He pointed at the word "*name*" in Matthew 28:19 and asked, "What is the name?" This question got me to thinking. Then he asked, "Did not our Lord say to His disciple Philip, 'he that hath seen me hath seen the Father?'"

> *Philip saith unto him, Lord show us the Father, and it sufficeth us. Jesus saith unto him, Have I been so long time with you, and yet hast thou not known me, Philip? He that hath seen me hath seen the Father; and how sayest thou then, show us the Father?* (John 14:8–9).

Further, Jesus said, "I am come in my Father's name, and ye receive me not: if another shall come in his own name, him ye will receive" (John 5:43). So, Jesus bears the name of the Father!

Then Brother and Sister Johnstone took me to another verse of Scripture where our Lord spoke of the name associated with the Holy Ghost:

> *But the Comforter, which is the Holy Ghost, whom the Father will send in my **name**, he shall teach you all things, and bring to your remembrance, whatsoever I have said unto you* (John 14:26).

Come Unto ME

Brother Johnstone explained further that he, too, was a son and a father, but his name was Johnstone. He went on to explain that our Lord is the Christ, our Lord is the Father, our Lord is the Holy Ghost, and that His **name** is *Jesus*. This explanation made perfect sense. All the understanding came together for me. There is no contradiction between Matthew 28:19 and Acts 2:38. The two Scriptures mean the same thing.

What is the one "name of the Father, and of the Son, and of the Holy Ghost"? Matthew 1:21 reveals the name of the Son was Jesus: "And she shall bring forth a son, and thou shalt call his name Jesus: for he shall save his people from their sins." John 5:43 indicates that Jesus bears the name of the Father. Further, the Holy Spirit came in Jesus' name, as well (John 14:26). Jesus is the one name of the Father, Son, and Holy Spirit.

Years later a young evangelist came to our church. I liked the way he explained the relationship between Matthew 28:19 and Acts 2:38. He simply stated that Matthew 28:19 is the command, and Acts 2:38 is the manifestation or fulfillment of the command. Jesus had taught His disciples how to carry out the water baptism. The Book of Acts is the documented proof of how the Apostles performed the baptism.

During the Bible study Brother Johnstone and his precious wife were giving me, the Lord was bringing Scriptures to my mind that I had been given as a child. In my Catholic training we were taught about the name Immanuel. Our Lord was also called *Immanuel*, which means "God with us." This means God Himself was manifested in the Child. This verse of Scripture now made sense. God was with us through Jesus Christ. Brother and Sister Johnstone were allowing the Holy Ghost to lead them through this home Bible study, bringing enlightenment of biblical truths to my understanding. They then led me to another verse of Scripture found in Isaiah:

The Apostle Peter and Water Baptism

> *For unto us a child is born, unto us a son is given: and the government shall be upon his shoulder: and his name shall be called Wonderful, The everlasting Father, the Prince of Peace* (Isaiah 9:6).

Therefore, the Christ Child is "the everlasting Father." He was born for the purpose of bringing redemption to humankind. Then I received another outstanding explanation in this Bible study. Brother Johnstone took me in Scripture to one of our Lord's last miracles. "But one of the soldiers with a spear pierced his side, and forthwith came there out blood and water" (John 19:34).

In the past I used to wonder about this verse of Scripture. The verse had come to me time and again from the Holy Ghost because I had often heard it read from our Catholic missalettes. Brother Johnstone explained that the water symbolized water baptism and that we have the covering of **Jesus' blood** through water baptism in Jesus' name. Here was the answer to a question I had been looking for. I had wondered, "What did it mean to be covered by the blood?" Being water baptized in Jesus' name gave me the covering of Jesus' blood. In the Book of Revelation, John meant such a covering when he stated, "And they overcame him by the blood of the Lamb, and by the word of their testimony" (Revelation 12:11).

So I went to church and was water baptized in the wonderful name of Jesus on December 1, 1996. Thank You so much, Jesus!

Therefore, we can share in the understanding of the apostles and share in the breathtaking experience of true salvation:

> *Then opened he their understanding, that they might understand the scriptures, And said unto them, Thus it is written, and thus it behooved Christ to suffer, and to rise from the dead the third day: And that repentance and re-*

mission of sins should be preached in his name among all nations, beginning at Jerusalem (Luke 24:45–47).

CHAPTER TEN
LIVING IN THE POWER OF THE SPIRIT

EACH and every one of us has a story. We all have had hurts in our lives, whether physical or emotional, and the scars often remain undetected in our hearts and minds. In our lifetimes, we experience pain, sorrow, disappointment, financial loss, or even illness. Whatever our situation, nearly every day we all experience discouragement. Many of us have even been to a variety of churches looking for purpose and a genuine relationship with the Lord. Some may wonder if God even exists at all. Yet when we are alone with our thoughts, some may wonder if they are going to make it to Heaven. The purpose in sharing my story is to help the reader to understand that a relationship with the Lord and His work in our lives by the Holy Spirit are very real. The Spirit of the Lord living within us is a glorious experience!

Some people who have never experienced the power of the Spirit may think, Well, but it looks strange, or odd, when the Holy Ghost moves on people in church services. One should not feel alone if that is how one first views Pentecostal worship. This is a commonly shared first impression of Pentecostal services to those who have never encountered Spirit-filled congregations. Many individuals in Pentecostal churches also experienced some of those thoughts at first. We must trust the leading of our heavenly Father and not put our trust in human wisdom or in our own thoughts. As is evident in the Scriptures, faith and trust are vital components of a genuine and vibrant relationship with God.

Come Unto ME

At that time Jesus answered and said, I thank thee, O Father, Lord of heaven and earth, because thou hast hid these things from the wise and prudent, and hast revealed them unto babes. Even so, Father: for so it seemed good in thy sight (Matthew 12:25–26).

Psalm 19:7 encourages believers to accept the Lord's testimony concerning His leadership: "The law of the LORD is perfect, converting the soul: the testimony of the LORD is sure, making wise the simple."

Our natural tendency is to trust our human knowledge and experience. However, I Corinthians 1:19–21 encourages to exercise faith and trust in God:

> *For it is written, I will destroy the wisdom of the wise, and will bring to nothing the understanding of the prudent. Where is the wise? Where is the scribe? Where is the disputer of this world? Hath not God made foolish the wisdom of this world? For after that in the wisdom of God the world by wisdom knew not God, it pleased God by the foolishness of preaching to save them that believe.*

Our human intellect and biases should not be our guide to a spiritual relationship with Jesus Christ, but that we simply believe God's Word and obey it. God desires to have a personal relationship with us, but we must exercise the simple, trusting faith of a child in order to draw near to Him. Jesus explained in Mark 10:15, "Verily I say unto you, Whosoever shall not receive the kingdom of God as a little child, he shall not enter therein."

For example, many individuals have been taught the outpouring of the Holy Ghost at Pentecost was only for the early days of the Feast of Pentecost, only to start the church. This biased teaching has caused some to trust more in their knowledge and fleshly intellect than to trust in God's Word. However, the Scriptures clearly reveal the outpouring of the Holy Ghost was not just for the Day of Pentecost; it is a powerful and redemptive experience that God has promised to all generations as explained in Acts 2:38–39:

> *Then Peter said unto them, Repent, and be baptized every one of you in the name of Jesus Christ for the remission of sins, and ye shall receive the gift of the Holy Ghost.* **For the promise is unto you, and your children, and to all that are afar off, even as many as the Lord our God shall call.**

If a person doubts the Word of God, he or she should repent and embrace the Word. I had to repent of my doubts and continue attending services until God revealed His Word to me and I received the Holy Spirit. A believer exercises faith in God's Word so he or she can experience the wonderful joy the Lord has available through the Holy Ghost. The joy, peace, and love one feels in his or her heart during the moment of receiving the Holy Spirit is difficult to express in words. All I can say is it is truly a most wonderful experience! "Joy Unspeakable" is a phrase and concept from Scripture (I Peter 1:8; Romans 14:17) as well as an old hymn often sung by Pentecostals. It says, "It is joy unspeakable, and full of glory." One could think of the happiest time of his or her life, and receiving the Spirit brings joy that is multiple times greater than anything he or she has ever experienced! Having the Holy Ghost also gives the believer power to witness:

> *But ye shall receive power, after that the Holy Ghost is come upon you: and ye shall be witnesses unto me both in Jerusalem, and in all Judæa, and in Samaria, and unto the uttermost part of the earth* (Acts 1:8).

However, the baptism of the Spirit is for far more than only to empower a person as a witness for God. The baptism of the Holy Ghost is our final seal to prepare us for Heaven as seen in Ephesians 4:30: "And grieve not the Holy Spirit of God, whereby ye are sealed unto the day of redemption." The baptism of the Spirit also empowers us to live a life above sin as Paul wrote to the Galatians:

> But the fruit of the Spirit is love, joy, peace, longsuffering, gentleness, goodness, faith, meekness, temperance: against such there is no law. And they that are Christ's have crucified the flesh with the affections and lusts (Galatians 5:22–24).

Many churches embrace the Apostle Peter's message of salvation: repentance, water baptism in Jesus' name for the forgiveness of sins, and receiving the baptism of the Holy Ghost as evidenced by speaking in other tongues. There are websites available that list multiple churches that believe and share this salvation message. Two of these are listed below, but there are many different organizations that also have websites, which will assist in guiding a person to a church that preaches this salvation message from the Book of Acts.

http://www.upci.com/church/locator/search

http://www.apostolic-churches.com

The significance of receiving the Holy Spirit and being baptized in water in the name of Jesus Christ for the remission of sins becomes even clearer and more powerful when we recognize the full and true identity of Jesus Christ. The following chapter introduces us to the biblical truths regarding the glorious identity and mission of Jesus Christ. What a privilege it is to be associated with Jesus through His name and Holy Spirit!

CHAPTER ELEVEN
NOT THREE GODS IN ONE, BUT ONE GOD IN CHRIST JESUS

IF you had to choose between embracing a theological idea that is clearly expressed in the Bible or choosing one with no fundamental basis in Scripture—one developed by theologians using history and human logic—which idea would you choose to embrace? Wouldn't we all want to accept the purely biblical doctrine over that which is taught by those who purport to interpret the Bible but who fail to correctly divide the Word of truth? I think so. Sadly, such is the very choice Christians must face between embracing the traditional, human idea of the Trinity versus the clear teachings of Scripture regarding the Oneness of God.

Many Christians today blindly accept the doctrine of the Trinity even though the word "trinity" does not appear in Scripture and its tenets are without biblical foundation. Unfortunately, many Christians have accepted the idea of a triune Godhead because it is the only doctrine about God's nature to which they have been exposed, but that does not make it biblically correct.

Being raised in a Catholic school, I clearly remember the entire class standing up while repeatedly chanting at the direction of the nun, "Three Gods in one." Years later as an adult and after receiving the baptism of the Holy Ghost, the teaching of "three Gods in one" began to trouble me. While I still believed in the idea of "three Gods in one," or the "Trinity" as many Christians call it, I began to wonder, *Should I worship each God, or each "person of the Godhead."* I have heard others with the baptism of the Holy Ghost who also wondered and struggled with the same question. I would contemplate, *If God is truly "three Gods in one," should I spend time with each "God" separately on a daily basis?* In time, I began to wonder if there were possibly something amiss with the "three-Gods-in-one" doctrine and whether something about that idea was causing me to experience confusion. My questions grew and emerged into several considerations:

- "Does God's nature portray the idea of a 'Threeness' or does His nature portray the idea of a 'Oneness'?"

- "Where did this idea of 'Three Gods in One' originate in history?"

- "Why was I taught 'God is three Gods'?"

- "Is God really 'Three Gods in One' or is He one God?"

- "What is the correct idea and understanding about God?"

I began searching the Bible for the word "Trinity," but the word "Trinity" was nowhere to be found in the Scriptures. Neither could I find anywhere in the four Gospels where Jesus taught His disciples to worship "Three separate Gods in One." However, I did find many verses of Scripture that appeared to teach the idea of One God who is omnipresent Spirit and who was manifested in Christ Jesus. For example, consider the words of Jesus teaching the Samaritan woman at the well:

> *Jesus saith unto her, Woman, believe me, the hour cometh, when ye shall neither in this mountain, nor yet at Jerusalem, worship the Father. Ye worship ye know not what: we know what we worship; for salvation is of the Jews. But the hour cometh, and now is, when the true worshippers shall worship the Father in spirit and in truth: for the Father seeketh such to worship him. God is a Spirit:*

Not Three Gods in One, but One God in Christ Jesus

*and they that worship him **must** worship him in spirit and in **truth*** (John 4:21–24).

These words of Jesus reached out to me, and the word **"truth"** especially caught my attention. Christ's words to the woman that we **must** worship both in Spirit and in **truth** made me determined to ascertain what the Lord actually meant by worshipping "in **truth**." Could this be why I was feeling conviction from the Spirit of God about this idea of a "threeness" in the Godhead, the Trinity doctrine, which I had been taught while growing up in the Catholic church? I was determined to study this idea of the Godhead—specifically, the Trinity—both in the Bible itself and in history, to find out when the Trinity doctrine actually began. First, we will start with an examination of the Scriptures and then we will search history.

Could I have been feeling in the Holy Spirit that I was not worshiping God "in truth" because I was worshiping God in a perceived "threeness" of a Trinity? I began searching the Old Testament. When I read again the Ten Commandments in full in the Book of Deuteronomy, I noticed the words:

> "Hear, O Israel: The LORD our **God is one LORD:** and thou shalt love the LORD thy God with all thine heart, and with all thy soul, and with all thy might" (Deuteronomy 6:4–5).

Deuteronomy 2:4 clearly indicates God is one, not three. We might question then, "How is it possible for God to be only one when He also reveals Himself through His son and through the Holy Ghost?" The answer exists in a truth also proclaimed by Jesus to the woman at the well: "God is a Spirit: and they that worship him must worship him in spirit and in truth" (John 4:24). This concept is key to understanding the nature of the Godhead. One cannot see or comprehend "spirit" unless that spirit is manifested in some visible, tangible form.

Come Unto ME

The only way we can perceive God, who is Spirit, is through a tangible manifestation. Paul made reference to this in his letter to Timothy:

> *"And without controversy great is the mystery of godliness: God was manifest in the flesh, justified in the Spirit, seen of angels, preached unto the Gentiles, believed on in the world, received up into glory"* (I Timothy 3:16).

Paul was clear that God (Spirit) manifested Himself on earth through the flesh of Jesus Christ, whom we refer to as the Son of God. The Scriptures do not indicate that His flesh was a separate being or a separate God; rather the Holy Spirit of God manifested Himself through the flesh of Jesus Christ. Another verse of Scripture reveals that even the devils understand there is only one God:

> *"Thou believest that there is one God; thou doest well: the devils also believe, and tremble"* (James 2:19).

If belief in "one God" causes fear and trembling among the devils, perhaps it is a vital truth about God that every believer also should understand and embrace. However, centuries of many Christians believing and promoting the idea of a Trinity has created many honest questions in the minds of believers. For example, individuals might ask the following questions:

- What causes individuals to be confused regarding the identity and nature of God?
- Why do many Christians think of God as three persons instead of one?
- To whom was Jesus praying in the Garden of Gethsemane?
- Was Jesus not praying to the Father?

Not Three Gods in One, but One God in Christ Jesus

All of these questions have a perfectly logical, biblical answer, none of which are difficult to understand to the honest and discerning student of Scripture. Discovering and understanding the answers, however, requires sincerity, an honest heart toward God, and beginning by establishing a foundation of a few fundamental truths about God and His nature.

1. *God is a Spirit* (John 4:24). A spirit does not have flesh and bones (Luke 24:39), but is incorporeal. The only way to visually comprehend a spirit is by that spirit manifesting itself in a visual, material way.

2. *God is eternal—without beginning or end* (Psalm 90:2; 93:2). See also Hebrews 1:10–12; 13:8; Revelation 1:8.

3. *God (eternal spirit) has manifested Himself unto us through several fundamental roles through which He has dealt with humankind:* (a) As the heavenly Father in Creation (eternal spirit creating, guiding, and directing the world and all that is therein); (b) As the Son of God in redemption (Jesus Christ, the Son, or flesh, of God, manifested for the purpose of paying the enormous price of human redemption). The Holy Spirit overshadowed Mary and caused a divine conception to occur (Matthew 1:18–23; Luke 1:35); consequently, the son Mary bore was both human and divine—truly unique and like no other one born throughout human history. Jesus Christ was truly the God-man, born for the purpose of human redemption—God manifested in human flesh; (c) As the Holy Spirit (Ghost) in regeneration (John 14:26; 16:7, 13; Luke 24:49; Acts 1:8, 13–15; 2:1–4, 12–40), leading and guiding believers into all truth.

4. *The only lasting, physical manifestation of God is the Son of God, Jesus Christ, born of the virgin Mary by the Holy Spirit's conception (John 1).*

Come Unto ME

In the beginning was the Word, and the Word was with God, and the Word was God. The same was in the beginning with God. All things were made by him; and without him was not any thing made that was made. In him was life; and the life was the light of men. . . . He was in the world, and the world was made by him, and the world knew him not. He came unto his own, and his own received him not. But as many as received him, to them gave he power to become the sons of God, even to them that believe on his name: Which were born, not of blood, nor of the will of the flesh, nor of the will of man, but of God. And the Word was made flesh, and dwelt among us, (and we beheld his glory, the glory as of the only begotten of the Father,) full of grace and truth. . . . No man hath seen God at any time; the only begotten Son, which is in the bosom of the Father, he hath declared him (John 1:1–18).

God, who at sundry times and in divers manners spake in time past unto the fathers by the prophets, hath in these last days spoken unto us by his Son, whom he hath appointed heir of all things, by whom also he made the worlds; Who being the brightness of his glory, and the express image of his person, and upholding all things by the word of his power, when he had by himself purged our sins, sat down on the right hand of the Majesty on high (Hebrews 1:1–3).

Jesus saith unto him, Have I been so long time with you, and yet hast thou not known me, Philip? he that hath seen me hath seen the Father; and how sayest thou then, Shew us the Father (John 14:9).

Not Three Gods in One, but One God in Christ Jesus

These verses of Scripture and many other verses pertaining to Jesus Christ reveal His identity as the fullness of God (Spirit) manifested in human flesh (as the Son of God). For example, John 1:18 specifically refers to the human body of Christ, the Son of God, which revealed or "declared" to humankind the eternal Spirit of God, or the heavenly Father. All these verses empower us to understand the deity of God in Christ Jesus and recognize the difference between the eternal Holy Spirit of God and the fleshly body of Christ, in whom dwelled all the fullness of God bodily (Colossians 1:19; 2:8–10).

> *Beware lest any man spoil you through philosophy and vain deceit, after the tradition of men, after the rudiments of the world, and not after Christ. For in him dwelleth all the fulness of the Godhead bodily. And ye are complete in him, which is the head of all principality and power* (Colossians 2:8–10).

God began to unfold the beauty of His identity in Christ Jesus both from the prophetic Messianic Scriptures of the Old Testament and from their fulfillment in the New Testament. Consider the Scriptures detailing the birth of Christ.

> *Now the birth of Jesus Christ was on this wise: When as his mother Mary was espoused to Joseph, before they came together, she was found with child of the Holy Ghost. Then Joseph her husband, being a just man, and not willing to make her a public example, was minded to put her away privily. But while he thought on these things, behold, the angel of the Lord appeared unto him in a dream, saying, Joseph, thou son of David, fear not to take unto thee Mary thy wife: for that which is conceived in her is of the Holy Ghost. And she shall bring forth a son, and thou shalt call his name Jesus: for he shall save his people from their sins.*

> *Now all this was done, that it might be fulfilled which was spoken of the Lord by the prophet, saying, Behold, a virgin shall be with child, and shall bring forth a son, and they shall call his name Emmanuel, which being interpreted is, God with us* (Matthew 1:18–23).

Jesus Christ is the only begotten Son of God. What does that mean? Begotten is an old word, which we find in the *King James Version* of Scripture, and which refers to Christ as the "begotten" Son of God. In the original Greek language of New Testament Scripture, we discover the word *begotten* simply means "born." In other words, only one time has the Holy Spirit of God departed from the usual and ordinary process of human conception and birth, which was in the case of the birth of the Son of God—the God-man born of the virgin Mary, born for the redemption of mankind. In other words, the Holy Spirit overshadowed Mary and caused her to conceive by divine and miraculous intervention, and Jesus Christ was born. The reason for this manifestation of divinity is clear: no human could ever pay the price for human sins, for every human is tainted by sin. So God (eternal Holy Spirit) robed Himself in human flesh, born that He might make the eternal sacrifice for sin. He alone was without the taint and corruption of sin, and He alone was qualified and capable to purchase our redemption.

In that the flesh of Christ was the begotten Son, Jesus was divinely anointed of God. *Christ* means "anointed One." Jesus was divinely anointed by the Holy Spirit that was within Him and guiding Him. Jesus Christ was fully human (born of Mary) and fully God (conceived by the Holy Spirit). Jesus was God manifested in the flesh with a heavenly anointing for ministry to humanity, concluding with His divine provision for salvation from sins. Because He was both human and divine, Jesus was both the Son of Man and the Son of God.

Not Three Gods in One, but One God in Christ Jesus

> *The Son of man must suffer many things, and be rejected of the elders and chief priests and scribes, and be slain, and be raised the third day* (Luke 9:22).

It is clear that when Jesus speaks of Himself as the Son of Man, He was speaking of His fleshly body. Christ's fleshly body was human and in His humanity He faced temptation just as we all are tempted. (See Matthew 4:1–11; Hebrews 4:15.) However, Jesus Christ successfully resisted temptation and He remained without sin all His human life. Consequently, He was qualified and willing to fulfill His divine mission and He was obedient to the plan of God, even unto death. As Jesus faced this time of great testing in the hours just prior to His crucifixion, He spent time in prayer in the garden of Gethsemane.

> *And he was withdrawn from them about a stone's cast, and kneeled down, and prayed, Saying, Father, if thou be willing, remove this cup from me: nevertheless not my will, but thine, be done* (Luke 22:41–42).

This glimpse of Christ praying to His heavenly Father just prior to His crucifixion has caused some to question, "To whom was Jesus praying?" "If Jesus is God manifested in the flesh, was He praying to Himself?" However, following our fundamental understanding of God from Scripture, we recognize that the prayers of Jesus involved the flesh of Christ, the man, praying to the eternal Spirit of God, which was manifested within and through Him. This was true of all the incidents recorded in Scripture that depict Jesus praying to the Father. Jesus had to subdue and conquer His human flesh in a way that is similar to how Christian believers pray and submit their fleshly will to the divine will of God in their lives. For example, see Jesus' prayer in Luke 10:21-22. Jesus demonstrated our need for prayer by Himself praying, subjugating His humanity to His deity.

When a person recognizes the uniqueness of Christ—God manifested in the flesh—it unfolds a divine understanding of many passages in the New Testament that otherwise would seem obscure and difficult to understand, at best. Consider the following examples.

Consider the dialog between Jesus and some of the religious leaders of His day as recorded in John 8:1-59. It is a lengthy chapter that depicts a conversation back and forth between Jesus and His detractors—the religious scribes and Pharisees. It began when they brought before Him a woman whom they had caught in the act of adultery. They really didn't care one way or another about the woman, but they wanted to try to entrap Jesus by how He might deal with the matter. The Law of Moses said she should be stoned, but Jesus came representing a higher law—the law of mercy and grace. Ultimately, Jesus forgave her and commanded her to go and depart from her sinful lifestyle. The conversation with the woman caught in adultery came to an abrupt end, but the dialog with the scribes and Pharisees continued off and on throughout the chapter, reaching a dramatic apex in verses 52-59.

> *Then said the Jews unto him, Now we know that thou hast a devil. Abraham is dead, and the prophets; and thou sayest, If a man keep my saying, he shall never taste of death. Art thou greater than our father Abraham, which is dead? and the prophets are dead: whom makest thou thyself? Jesus answered, If I honour myself, my honour is nothing: it is my Father that honoureth me; of whom ye say, that he is your God: Yet ye have not known him; but I know him: and if I should say, I know him not, I shall be a liar like unto you: but I know him, and keep his saying.*

Not Three Gods in One, but One God in Christ Jesus

> *Your father Abraham rejoiced to see my day: and he saw it, and was glad. Then said the Jews unto him, Thou art not yet fifty years old, and hast thou seen Abraham? Jesus said unto them, Verily, verily, I say unto you, Before Abraham was, I am. Then took they up stones to cast at him: but Jesus hid himself, and went out of the temple, going through the midst of them, and so passed by.*

The scribes and Pharisees questioned Jesus' statements; they observed that Jesus was not even fifty years old. How could He have seen Abraham? Jesus' response seemed almost arcane and cryptic, and yet they clearly understood His meaning. Jesus said, *"Verily, verily, I say unto you, Before Abraham was, I am" (John 8:58)*. Compare Jesus' words with those of God spoken to Moses in Exodus 3:13–14: "And Moses said unto God, Behold, when I come unto the children of Israel, and shall say unto them, The God of your fathers hath sent me unto you; and they shall say to me, What is his name? what shall I say unto them? And God said unto Moses, I AM THAT I AM: and he said, Thus shalt thou say unto the children of Israel, I AM hath sent me unto you" (Exodus 3:13–14). In the Old Testament, the people of God knew Him as the Great I AM. Although it seemed to be a strange name, it was a verb of continuous, present being. It aptly described God for He had no beginning and will have no ending; He is eternally existent in the present tense: I AM. Consequently, when Jesus said, "Before Abraham was [past tense], I am [present tense]," the Jewish audience understood perfectly the implication of Jesus' words and they were ready to stone Him (John 8:59)! Jesus was clearly identifying Himself as the "Great I AM."

There were multiple times in the New Testament in which Jesus identified Himself as the Almighty. One can read a similar passage in John 10:23–31:

> And Jesus walked in the temple in Solomon's porch. Then came the Jews round about him, and said unto him, How long dost thou make us to doubt? If thou be the Christ, tell us plainly. Jesus answered them, I told you, and ye believed not: the works that I do in my Father's name, they bear witness of me. But ye believe not, because ye are not of my sheep, as I said unto you. My sheep hear my voice, and I know them, and they follow me: And I give unto them eternal life; and they shall never perish, neither shall any man pluck them out of my hand. My Father, which gave them me, is greater than all; and no man is able to pluck them out of my Father's hand. I and my Father are one. Then the Jews took up stones again to stone him.

It is clear in this passage that Jesus Christ was intimating complete Oneness with the Father. He was not just claiming to be in unison with God, but He was God. He could only make such claims because He *was the eternal God robed in human flesh.* He possessed unity with the heavenly Father because He was God robed in flesh. Jesus often identified Himself with the Father. Consider His dialog with Philip:

> Philip saith unto him, Lord, shew us the Father, and it sufficeth us. Jesus saith unto him, Have I been so long time with you, and yet hast thou not known me, Philip? he that hath seen me hath seen the Father; and how sayest thou then, Shew us the Father? Believest thou not that I am in the Father, and the Father in me? the words that I speak unto you I speak not of myself: but the Father that dwelleth in me, he doeth the works (John 14:8–10).

Jesus was speaking as the only One in whom dwelled all the fullness of God bodily. Jesus clearly revealed that the only way Philip

Not Three Gods in One, but One God in Christ Jesus

could see the Father was by seeing Him. Jesus Christ is the visible image of the invisible God (Hebrews 1:3; Colossians 1:15).

> *Who hath delivered us from the power of darkness, and hath translated us into the kingdom of his dear Son: In whom we have redemption through his blood, even the forgiveness of sins: Who is the image of the invisible God, the firstborn of every creature: For by him were all things created, that are in heaven, and that are in earth, visible and invisible, whether they be thrones, or dominions, or principalities, or powers: all things were created by him, and for him: And he is before all things, and by him all things consist. And he is the head of the body, the church: who is the beginning, the firstborn from the dead; that in all things he might have the preeminence. For it pleased the Father that in him should all fulness dwell* (Colossians 1:13–10).

In Colossians 1:13–19, which is clearly speaking of the Son of God (verse 13–14), Jesus made several references to His identity as God:

Jesus is the image of the invisible God (verse 15);

- Jesus acted as the Creator of all things (verse 16);
- Jesus made all things for Himself (verse 16);
- Jesus was before all things (verse 17);
- Through Jesus all things hold together, or "consist" (verse 17);
- Jesus is the head of the church (verse 18);
- Jesus has the preeminence in all things (verse 18);
- In Jesus dwells all the fullness of the Father (verse 19; 2:9).

Clearly, Jesus Christ is the Father manifested in human flesh!

Further, Jesus Christ has "all power" in heaven and in earth: "And Jesus came and spake unto them, saying, All power is given unto me in heaven and in earth" (Matthew 28:18). To this proclamation of Jesus, Trinitarians often will say, "See! I caught you! Jesus said 'all power was given' to Him. He had to receive it from another entity." However, to that response I just smile and ask, "So, if there is another person besides Jesus—One who gave Jesus all the power—how much power is left for that entity?" The obvious answer is "None." Clearly, *Jesus Christ has all power in heaven and in earth, leaving no power or authority for any other, deity or otherwise.*

If there is any deity other than that manifested in and through Jesus Christ, he did not create anything, nothing was created for him, and he is absolutely impotent—without power—for Jesus Christ possesses all power, made all things, and made those things for Himself! (See Matthew 28:18; Colossians 1:13–19.)

It is a matter of understanding that Jesus was both fully human and fully God; He was not just a man in whom the Holy Spirit dwelled. He was and is God manifested in flesh. That represents a significant distinction! One must recognize the dual nature of Christ—human and divine. One must further recognize that He spoke both as man and as God. As a man, He could say "all power is given unto me," for He recognized the power and purpose of God at work through the Incarnation, which means the manifestation of God in flesh. Jesus was more than just a man! We should understand His dual nature and the distinction that existed between the two natures, though they were seamlessly joined in the Son of God:

- As a man, Christ ate; as God He multiplied the loaves and the fishes.

Not Three Gods in One, but One God in Christ Jesus

- As a man, Christ became weary and slept; as God He awoke and calmed the seas that were threatening the ship on which they were sailing.

- As a man, He wept at the death of His friend, Lazarus; as God He spoke, raised Lazarus from death, and called him to come forth from the tomb where he had been bound and laid.

- As a man, He prayed in the Garden, "Father, if possible, let this cup pass from me; As God, however, He arose determined to proceed with His holy purpose in securing the redemption for all humankind through the Cross.

- Notice several other clues to the Oneness of God that were visible through the writings of the Old Testament prophets:

- God identified Himself as the Savior: "For I am the Lord thy God, the Holy One of Israel, thy Savior" (Isaiah 43:3).

- The Lord clearly revealed He is the only Savior: "I, even I, am the Lord; and beside me there is no savior" (Isaiah 43:11).

- There is no other Savior other than the almighty God: "Yet I am the Lord thy God from the land of Egypt, and thou shalt know no god but me: for there is no savior beside me" (Hosea 13:4).

There are many more verses of Scripture in the Old Testament that refer to God as the One true and only God and the only sovereign Savior of humankind. In Jesus Christ dwelled all the fullness of the Almighty—God incarnate as the Son of God. The Son of God is the only begotten son, born for the purpose of human salvation. Jesus was not a second of three gods in one Godhead, nor the second person of the Godhead. Rather, all the fullness of the Godhead dwelt fully in Him. Further, the name Jesus is derived from the Hebrew name Yeshua, (or Joshua, the English spelling) which also is Iesous in the Greek (or Jesus, the English spelling). However one spells or pronounces the name, His name means "The Lord is salvation" or "The Lord has become salvation."

In other words, God was manifested in flesh through Jesus Christ that He might become our salvation. Without His intervention we would have no hope of salvation, but through Him we can be saved. Jesus is the Lamb of God slain from the foundation of the world for our sins as a sin offering. (See Revelation 13:8.) In other words, from the beginning God had a plan (from the foundation of the world) to provide the supreme sacrifice necessary for the redemption of mankind.

Once again, it is important to emphasize the dual nature of Christ and the distinction between the two. When Christ died on the cross, God did not die; the man Christ Jesus died. God cannot die for it is impossible. This is the reason why we witness Jesus in a great fleshly struggle as He neared death and cried out, "Eli, Eli, lama sabachthani? that is to say, My God, my God, why hast thou forsaken me" (Matthew 27:46). This was the reaction of the man, Christ Jesus, when the Spirit of God withdrew from Him. The Spirit had to withdraw, for Christ could not die as long as He remained God in human flesh. God withdrew long enough to allow the body of Christ to die, thereby providing the necessary sacrificial death on the Cross. However, after three days, just as Jesus had promised, He resurrected from the dead.

> *Jesus answered and said unto them, Destroy this temple, and in three days I will raise it up. Then said the Jews, Forty and six years was this temple in building, and wilt thou rear it up in three days? But he spake of the temple of his body* (John 2:19–21).

Not Three Gods in One, but One God in Christ Jesus

Jesus promised to raise Himself from the dead in three days; He needed no other power to resurrect from death beyond that which He possessed as the Almighty. His robe of humanity did not limit or prevent His power and authority of deity.

In history, the term and idea of a Trinity was unknown to the Apostles and early believers. Further, there is no real hint of Trinitarian ideology in the Scriptures; the verses Trinitarians use to try to support their theology are actually misunderstandings that are the result of failing to fully comprehend the dual nature of God exhibited in the Incarnation.

According to David K. Bernard in his work *Oneness and Trinity, AD 100–300*, "In the beginning of the third century we find the first clearly identifiable trinitarian language. The person most responsible for the development of trinitarianism in its earliest stage was Tertullian, the first major theologian to write in Latin" (*Oneness and Trinity, AD 100–300*, Bernard, p. 105). Tertullian, along with the influence of Origen, Clement, and other theologians developed the idea of the Trinity over the next hundred years. Finally, the doctrine of the Trinity was adopted at the Council of Nicea in AD 325 and further refined at the Council of Constantinople in AD 381.

The real point concerning the development of the doctrine of the Trinity historically is that it was developed by men over at least the span of a century. Further, the Apostles and those closest to Jesus Christ knew no such doctrine. Their writings, which comprise most of the New Testament, clearly declare the Oneness of God as manifested and revealed in Christ Jesus for our redemption. We can choose to accept the ideas of men or we can by faith embrace the writings of Scripture—penned by men who were inspired to write by the Holy Spirit. These were men who knew and walked with Jesus Christ on earth.

Come Unto ME

The choice is ours to make, but the Lord and His apostles did not teach an idea of God in a "Threeness" or the doctrine of a Trinity. Such an idea about God developed later, was extra-biblical, and was not taught by the early church.

It is vital to avoid this and other misconceptions about salvation and the Word of God. Nothing should be more important to us than to know the pure truths of the Holy Bible and to experience the precious and glorious redemption provided by our Savior.

CHAPTER TWELVE
AVOIDING COMMON MISCONCEPTIONS ABOUT SALVATION

WHEN I was visiting various churches in my ten years of searching for the truth of salvation, I encountered many other false doctrines and ideas claiming to be the truth. One major false doctrine I discovered appeared to be very popular in many Christian churches: "the Roman road to salvation." First, I will attempt to explain the teaching and then share what I have learned about the concept. Those who promote the idea of the Roman road to salvation take their idea of the salvation plan from just one verse of Scripture, Romans 10:9. Paul wrote, "That if thou shalt confess with thy mouth the Lord Jesus, and shalt believe in thine heart that God hath raised him from the dead, thou shalt be saved."

This verse of Scripture had bewildered me for several years. If that Scripture were the only verse of Scripture to be used in leading a person to salvation, why does their doctrine present so many misconceptions about redemption? I have listed below the many questions that occurred to me concerning the use of that sole verse of Scripture in the Book of Romans as a plan of salvation.

1. If all we needed to do in order to experience salvation were to simply believe on Jesus Christ as our Lord and Savior, why then was Christ water baptized in the Jordan River by John the Baptist? Certainly, I am not greater than Christ that

I should avoid water baptism, especially since Peter commanded it (Acts 2:38). The majority of churches state that water baptism is no longer essential for salvation. There indeed must be something wrong with this Roman road.

2. If receiving the Holy Spirit was not part of redemption, why were the early-church believers being baptized in the Holy Ghost? It couldn't have been just for the Day of Pentecost to anoint the Apostles to preach because they were baptizing new saints throughout the entire Book of Acts and these new believers were receiving the Holy Spirit just as on the Day of Pentecost.

3. If water baptism and receiving the Spirit were non-essential or not important, why are there multiple Scriptures throughout the Book of Acts regarding water baptism and the baptism of the Holy Ghost?

4. If water baptism is no longer of any effect, why did Paul write in Romans 6:3, "Know ye not, that so many of us as were baptized into Jesus Christ were baptized into his death?"

5. If we are no longer to be baptized in the Holy Spirit, why did Paul also write in Romans 4:9, "But ye are not in the flesh, but in the Spirit, if so be that the Spirit of God dwell in you. Now if any man have not the Spirit of Christ, he is none of his"?

6. Why did our Lord Jesus tell Nicodemus we must be born again of water and the Spirit to enter into the kingdom of God (John 3:5)? Am I going to choose to ignore or discount our Lord's own words?

7. If all that is necessary for salvation is that one believe on Jesus Christ, why did the Apostle Paul preach repentance and

Avoiding Common Misconceptions about Salvation

water baptism throughout the Book of Acts? (For example, see Acts 19:1–6.)

8. Are we to believe that in Romans 10:9 Paul was contradicting the Apostle Peter's message as recorded in Acts 2:38, or making it of no effect? If one carefully reads Acts 2, he or she will notice the question asked by the Jews who came to believe that Jesus was indeed their Messiah: "What shall we do?" (Acts 2:37). The Apostle Peter responded, "Repent, and be baptized every one of you in the name of Jesus Christ for the remission of sins, and ye shall receive the gift of the Holy Ghost" (Acts 2:38).

9. If professing Christians in other churches were truly saved by just believing, why are many of them continuing to live in sin? Doesn't the Bible state in Matthew 1:21 that Jesus came to save us *from* our sins and not *in* our sins? After all, isn't the whole basis of the Christian life to help us live a life without sin and to help us love God until the day He comes to take us home? Doesn't continuing to live in sin contradict Paul's teaching in Romans 6:1–2, where he stated, "What shall we say then? Shall we continue in sin, that grace may abound? God forbid. How shall we, that are dead to sin, live any longer therein?"

10. How is it that many Christian churches state they are saved by believing on Christ, yet many of their writers write books condemning Catholics for their practices? After all, Catholics believe that Jesus is Lord and Savior. If it were true that all anyone needed to do to be saved is to just believe on Christ as Lord, then why point a finger at Catholics or any other professing Christians who believe on Christ but who observe other religious practices and traditions?

These and many other questions plagued me and discouraged me from accepting the idea of the Roman road to salvation. Let me attempt to answer these questions more fully in the next paragraphs.

First, let's begin with the "Epistle of Paul the Apostle to the Romans." Here, I've spelled out the full name of this book of the Bible. One might be thinking, *Why is this significant?* Although we commonly call these "books" of the Bible, notice that Paul's writing was not written first as a *book*, but as an *epistle*. An epistle is a letter. Paul wrote a letter to the believers within an existing church congregation in Rome. These were individuals who had already experienced the plan of salvation as first given in the Book of Acts, which Peter had preached and which is recorded in Acts 2:38. A person should read the entire Book of Romans to observe and understand its full meaning. When reading Romans 2, readers will notice Paul was writing to an audience of Jewish believers. The early church was being plagued by Jews coming into the congregations attempting to lead the Jewish believers away from the gospel by promoting the necessity of circumcision in order to be saved. Consequently, the Apostle Paul addressed circumcision at the end of chapter 2, in the beginning of chapter 3, and throughout chapter 4 in his epistle to the Romans.

Consider once again Romans 10:9, a verse of Scripture upon which many Christian churches base their entire plan of salvation: "That if thou shalt confess with thy mouth the Lord Jesus and shalt believe in thine heart that God hath raised him from the dead, thou shalt be saved."

The majority of the Jews did not believe Jesus was the Messiah. However, it was essential they first demonstrate their faith in Christ by embracing Jesus as the Messiah before they could effectively follow through the rest of God's plan of salvation through repentance, water baptism in Jesus' name, and receiving the Holy Ghost. Faith

Avoiding Common Misconceptions about Salvation

is fundamentally essential to repentance, water baptism, and Spirit baptism. All people must first believe in Jesus Christ. Only then is one able to fully pursue the biblical plan for redemption and experience salvation.

For example, I have Christian friends who were former Jews who cry and mourn because their Jewish relatives do not believe Jesus Christ is the Messiah. This sorrow is understood when one reads Romans 11 where Paul wrote of the Jews who did not believe Jesus Christ was the Son of God and what happened to them because of their disbelief. Yet even now, if the Jewish people will believe, they can reclaim a place in the body of Christ.

For all believers—Jewish or Gentile—salvation is possible only through faith in Jesus Christ, repentance of sins, water baptism in the name of Jesus, and receiving the Holy Ghost. If we believe in Jesus Christ as Lord, then we can proceed to demonstrate our faith through obedience to the plan of salvation as preached by the Apostle Peter in Acts 2:38.

Paul also wrote in Romans 8:9, "Now if any man have not the Spirit of Christ, he is none of his." Paul was speaking of receiving the baptism of the Holy Spirit. Having the Holy Spirit is essential to redemption.

Taking a single verse of Scripture out of context is dangerous, which is what some individuals do with Romans 10:9. Paul was correct in writing to the Romans of the necessity of believing on the Lord Jesus Christ for salvation, but he was not suggesting that believing was the conclusion of our salvation; it is only the beginning. Belief on Jesus is the impetus to motivate us to pursue the full plan of redemption. We must read and obey the Scriptures in full and not selectively obey only the verses of our choosing. Paul did not contradict the preached message of Peter on the Day of Pentecost.

Come Unto ME

Reading and studying the Bible clarified in my own mind the Scriptures pertaining to Christ's own water baptism, of Jesus telling Nicodemus we must be born of water and Spirit to enter the kingdom of Heaven, and of many other verses of Scripture pertaining to God's redemptive plan. Paul did not write his epistle to the Romans years later to change the plan of salvation, but to reach out to encourage Jewish believers concerning the role of faith in the redemptive plan. It is vital we understand God's plan of salvation clearly.

Understanding how all the Scriptures fit together without contradiction helped me greatly to understand God's plan of salvation. After all, I needed to be delivered from false teachings I had learned at some churches. It also helped me to have a great sense of love and compassion for Catholics who believe as I once believed. Consequently, I was troubled greatly that some of the books I had read condemned Catholics for their practices. Although I have learned that many of those practices are unbiblical, I have compassion for those who continue in the Catholic church and I can see no constructive purpose in Christians offering wholesale condemnation of Catholics. Rather, Christian believers should reach out to Catholics with love and compassion, offering truth to them and allowing them to embrace truth for themselves, without condemnation.

It seemed inconsistent that these Christians would so readily condemn Catholics, who believed on Jesus Christ, while preaching a message of only believing on Jesus and rejecting the necessity of obeying Peter's message in Acts 2:38. If their message of "Just believe in Jesus" was a surety to salvation, then all would be saved—no matter the differences in belief. If all anyone needed to do was simply to believe, why condemn anyone else? Since I did not understand this inconsistency, I set out to pray and fast and seek understanding.

Avoiding Common Misconceptions about Salvation

After many days of prayer and fasting, an answer came to me. The answer was quite startling: many of the Christian churches had enslaved some of God's people with an incomplete message of salvation and a condemnatory spirit toward others who differed from them. It became clear to me that these churches had selectively chosen one verse of Scripture out of context to arrange for themselves a simplistic and incomplete "plan of salvation." We should refuse to allow anyone to enslave us spiritually or deceive us with an incomplete plan of salvation. Let us choose to follow the Apostles' plan of salvation from the Book of Acts.

I spent ten years going from church to church seeking preaching that would reflect the preaching of the Apostles. I believe it took ten years because many individuals had changed the Apostles' teachings over the course of 2,000 years of history. Moreover, in those ten years I suffered many things while on my search. I am sharing my experiences in an effort to save the readers from making many of the same mistakes and enduring the same sufferings as I endured. Some people learn best from reading of the experiences of others. I hope I have saved some individuals the heartache of trying to find truth without their having to blindly walk into a church with no knowledge of its doctrine.

Many churches continue to preach the Apostolic doctrines of Scripture. They recognize that the salvation message preached by Peter has not changed. As he preached in Acts 2, the message of redemption is still repentance of sins, water baptism in the name of Jesus for the remission of sins, and receiving the baptism of the Holy Ghost. Further, the message is for all people everywhere, as many as the Lord Jesus shall call:

> *For the promise is unto you, and to your children, and to all that are afar off, even as many as the Lord our God shall call* (Acts 2:39).

CHAPTER THIRTEEN
FULL SALVATION ENDURING TO THE END

TRUTH or tradition? Which will bring salvation to an individual?

There are many traditions of every sort in every tribe and culture around the world. Some of those traditions are biblical; some are unbiblical. Some traditions are good and some are bad. This being the case, it seems clear that traditions are not the source or basis of salvation.

Truth, however, involves known and established facts, whether known by scientific observation or accepted by faith. Hence, faith propels us to embrace God's Word, the Bible, as truth. The writers of Scripture testify of its identity and fundamental essence as being "truth."

Sanctify them through thy truth: thy word is truth (John 17:17).

> *For this cause also thank we God without ceasing, because, when ye received the word of God which ye heard of us, ye received it not as the word of men, but as it is in truth, the word of God, which effectually worketh also in you that believe* (I Thessalonians 2:13).

> *Study to shew thyself approved unto God, a workman that needeth not to be ashamed, rightly dividing the word of truth* (II Timothy 2:15).

Further, the Word of God proclaims the Spirit of God to be truth, and Jesus Christ to be truth.

> *This is he that came by water and blood, even Jesus Christ; not by water only, but by water and blood. And it is the Spirit that beareth witness, because the Spirit is truth* (I John 5:6).
>
> *Jesus saith unto him, I am the way, the truth, and the life: no man cometh unto the Father, but by me* (John 14:6).

Truth is a fundamental characteristic of God. In other words, it is impossible for God to speak a lie; truth is part of His character. Paul wrote of God's inability to lie in his epistle to Titus, and also in his epistle to the Romans. "In hope of eternal life, which God, that cannot lie, promised before the world began" (Titus 1:2). "Let God be true, but every man a liar" (Romans 3:4).

According to *Merriam-Webster Dictionary,* the definition of *truth* is "the truth: the real facts about something: the things that are true: the quality or state of being true: a statement or idea that is true or accepted as true."

The truth of God's Word is the basis upon which humankind may discover the plan and means for redemption from sin. Traditions may come and go; traditions may change. But truth is steady and constant—unchanging—and it is the only basis for salvation.

Because the Bible is truth and the only source for discovering and implementing salvation from sin, it is vital we study and follow its life-changing teachings. It is fine to have and follow traditions as long as they do not run counter to or interfere with the teachings of Scripture, but we cannot rely on traditions to save us. Only the truths of God's Word have redemptive power and authority.

So the question arises, "Why would an individual place his or her traditions above the clear teachings of Scripture?" Does such a

Full Salvation Enduring to the End

person have so little regard for his or her eternal destiny as to place human practices and traditions above God, His Word, and His will? Does that person not believe in an eternal Heaven and eternal hell? An old chorus written by Doug Davis comes to mind when I am thinking of my eternal destiny. The first line of the chorus states:

Above all else, I must be saved.

What could possibly be more important than ensuring our eternal salvation? In eternity, the preservation of human pride will be worthless; the value of human ideas and traditions will disappear; the stubbornness of human resolve will be powerless. The only thing that will matter in eternity is whether we obeyed the will of God as communicated through His Word, the Bible.

At the birth of the early church on the Day of Pentecost, God anointed Peter to stand and declare the inaugural message of the church, revealing His plan for human redemption:

Then Peter said unto them, Repent, and be baptized every one of you in the name of Jesus Christ for the remission of sins, and ye shall receive the gift of the Holy Ghost. For the promise is unto you, and to your children, and to all that are afar off, even as many as the Lord our God shall call. And with many other words did he testify and exhort, saying, Save yourselves from this untoward generation (Acts 2:38–40).

The only plan ever given to the church for salvation first involves faith, for only on the basis of belief in Jesus Christ is there a foundation for responding to the gospel. With obedient faith in Christ we then are commanded to repent of our sins. Repentance is a change of directions; it is turning away from our sinful past and turning toward God with a desire to please and serve Him in all we do, making our life a living sacrifice unto Him.

Come Unto ME

Peter then commanded that we be baptized in water in the name of Jesus Christ for the remission of sins. Our response to this command also involves faith, believing that His name will cleanse us from all iniquity as we die to our will and devote ourselves unreservedly unto His will and plan for our lives.

> *And now why tarriest thou? arise, and be baptized, and wash away thy sins, calling on the name of the Lord* (Acts 22:16).

Peter further promised we would receive the Holy Ghost, which is evidenced by speaking with other tongues as the Spirit gives the utterance. (See Acts 2:1–4, 38.) Just as the believers received the Spirit on the Day of Pentecost, we will receive the Holy Spirit, which seals our covenant with Christ and is the earnest (down payment) of our eternal inheritance. (See II Corinthians 1:22; 5:5; Ephesians 1:14.)

Jesus promised that when we receive the Holy Ghost He will "guide" us "into all truth." The Spirit empowers us to live a godly, overcoming Christian life in this fallen world infected by sin. The Spirit will open our understanding to the Scriptures and fill us with divine power to live for Christ and testify of His grace and glory.

> *Howbeit when he, the Spirit of truth, is come, he will guide you into all truth: for he shall not speak of himself; but whatsoever he shall hear, that shall he speak: and he will shew you things to come* (John 16:13).

> *But ye shall receive power, after that the Holy Ghost is come upon you: and ye shall be witnesses unto me both in Jerusalem, and in all Judaea, and in Samaria, and unto the uttermost part of the earth* (Acts 1:8).

Full Salvation Enduring to the End

In this life we will encounter troubles, trials, and tribulation, but the Holy Spirit within us empowers us to face every hardship and painful circumstance with faith in Christ and victory through His name. Jesus told us we will have tribulation just as He suffered tribulation, but that we should not fear for He has overcome the world (John 16:33). Our hope of experiencing patience and victory through every trial, tribulation, or stressful situation is anchored to our redemptive relationship with Jesus Christ. He will sustain and help us.

There are many countries today where Christians are experiencing severe persecution. However, even in countries where its citizens enjoy freedom of religion, there often is persecution of various sorts. Sometimes in America we suffer prejudice against Christianity and resulting measures of limited persecution. Further, one may experience tribulation and persecution within his or her own home because of sincere efforts to live pleasing to God. It is unfortunate, but many Christians endure suffering.

I experienced this kind of persecution. When coming in from a prayer meeting, my spouse would be hiding behind the door. He would knock me down, drag me up the stairs by my ankles, and throw me through the air against a wall. After I would hit the floor, my Bible would come flying, hit the wall, and land on the floor beside me. My spouse would stand on my chest while wildly screaming, "Do you think the world is about to come to an end?" I'd respond in a whisper, "Yes, and I'm going to get ready." However, I never missed a prayer meeting even though I knew what would happen when I returned home.

The Apostle Paul also suffered many horrible trials. He wrote of many of his experiences in his second epistle to the believers in Corinth:

> *Of the Jews five times received I forty stripes save one. Thrice was I beaten with rods, once was I stoned, thrice I suffered shipwreck, a night and a day I have been in the deep; in journeyings often, in perils of waters, in perils of robbers, in perils by mine own countrymen, in perils by the heathen, in perils in the city, in perils in the wilderness, in perils in the sea, in perils among false brethren; in weariness and painfulness, in watchings often, in hunger and thirst, in fastings often, in cold and nakedness* (II Corinthians 11:24–27).

Some believers naively think when they come to God life will hold no more problems. God never promised us a life without troubles or suffering. Our living, growing relationship with Jesus Christ through the indwelling Holy Spirit does not isolate us from trouble; rather, it inoculates us with faith and spiritual power that we may endure persecution and trials.

> *There hath no temptation taken you but such as is common to man: but God is faithful, who will not suffer you to be tempted above that ye are able; but will with the temptation also make a way to escape, that ye may be able to bear it* (I Corinthians 10:13).

Notice Paul's admonition to the Corinthians in I Corinthians 10:13. He assured them God would be faithful to provide "a way to escape, that ye may be able to bear it." He promised a way of escape, not avoidance. We cannot escape from that which we never enter or encounter. That is the reason Paul assured them God would empower them so they would "be able to bear it." God will support and sustain us through our times of suffering and lead us out of them victoriously.

Full Salvation Enduring to the End

Paul had faith in God. He knew life would bring difficult times, but he also knew it was working for his ultimate and eternal glory. He wrote to the Corinthians, "For which cause we faint not; but though our outward man perish, yet the inward man is renewed day by day. For our light affliction, which is but for a moment, worketh for us a far more exceeding and eternal weight of glory; while we look not at the things which are seen, but at the things which are not seen: for the things which are seen are temporal; but the things which are not seen are eternal" (II Corinthians 4:16–18). Paul's attitude always looked forward toward his eternal reward:

> *For to me to live is Christ, and to die is gain. But if I live in the flesh, this is the fruit of my labour: yet what I shall choose I wot not. For I am in a strait betwixt two, having a desire to depart, and to be with Christ; which is far better: Nevertheless to abide in the flesh is more needful for you. And having this confidence, I know that I shall abide and continue with you all for your furtherance and joy of faith* (Philippians 1:21–25).

Jesus clearly warned His disciples of the conflict they would encounter because of following Him. Further, He revealed that conflicts often would arise even within our own families. It is exceptionally painful to have to oppose our loved ones, but if we must choose between our loved ones and Jesus Christ, we should wisely choose our Savior.

> *Whosoever therefore shall confess me before men, him will I confess also before my Father which is in heaven. But whosoever shall deny me before men, him will I also deny before my Father which is in heaven. Think not that I am come to send peace on earth: I came not to send peace, but a sword. For I am come to set a man at variance against*

> *his father, and the daughter against her mother, and the daughter in law against her mother in law. And a man's foes shall be they of his own household. He that loveth father or mother more than me is not worthy of me: and he that loveth son or daughter more than me is not worthy of me. And he that taketh not his cross, and followeth after me, is not worthy of me. He that findeth his life shall lose it: and he that loseth his life for my sake shall find it* (Matthew 10:32–39).

When we, in faith, give ourselves to Jesus Christ through repentance of past sins and we submit to water baptism in Jesus' name for the remission of sins, we take the first steps toward enjoying a glorious and growing relationship with the blessed Savior. He fills us with His Spirit to redeem us, as a seal of our new life in Him, and as a source of spiritual strength and power that we may live in victory. As we walk with Christ, He leads and guides our steps by His indwelling Holy Spirit and He empowers us with a growing spiritual relationship. Further, He gives us strength to face the challenges and difficulties of life on earth.

Receiving the Holy Ghost is not the conclusion of our redemption; rather, it is only the beginning. It is the beginning of our growing, intimate relationship with the Savior of the world. We have Christ's assurance of salvation as long as we continue to walk with Him in obedient faith, endeavoring to follow the guidance of His Spirit and Word in our lives. We will encounter opposition and persecution in this life, but if we endure to the end we shall be saved.

> *And ye shall be hated of all men for my name's sake: but he that endureth to the end shall be saved* (Matthew 10:22).

Paul wrote to the Corinthians of their salvation through the gospel and the contingency that would ensure their salvation in the end:

Full Salvation Enduring to the End

"Moreover, brethren, I declare unto you the gospel which I preached unto you, which also ye have received, and wherein ye stand; by which also ye are saved, if ye keep in memory what I preached unto you, unless ye have believed in vain" (I Corinthians 15:1–2). According to Paul, the only thing that assures ultimate redemption is our keeping in memory—and practicing—the spiritual truths disseminated by Paul and his fellow writers of Scripture.

We must love God's Word and in faith follow its precepts as the Holy Spirit empowers us. As long as we keep our faith anchored in Jesus Christ and follow as He leads us, there is no power that can separate us from our relationship with Him.

> *Who shall separate us from the love of Christ? shall tribulation, or distress, or persecution, or famine, or nakedness, or peril, or sword? As it is written, For thy sake we are killed all the day long; we are accounted as sheep for the slaughter. Nay, in all these things we are more than conquerors through him that loved us. For I am persuaded, that neither death, nor life, nor angels, nor principalities, nor powers, nor things present, nor things to come, nor height, nor depth, nor any other creature, shall be able to separate us from the love of God, which is in Christ Jesus our Lord* (Romans 8:35–39).

I have prayed for you as I wrote and worked on this book. I have prayed God would strengthen you and empower you by His Spirit to follow Him, whatever the cost. I have prayed you will have courage and strength to endure whatever measures of persecution you may encounter. And, I have prayed that whatever the cost, you will choose to follow Christ and His Word. In the final analysis of life—when all is said and done and earthly life for us has ended—the only thing that will matter is God's opinion of us, which will involve how we accepted and followed His eternal Word.

INDEX

A
a different language *14*
Advocatrix *27*
Apostle *44, 65, 66, 67, 72, 82, 102, 103, 104, 105, 113*
apostles' doctrine *71*
Paul *44, 65, 69, 82, 86, 101, 102, 103, 104, 105, 106, 110, 113, 114, 115, 116, 117*
Peter *23, 46, 47, 50, 65, 66, 67, 68, 69, 72, 73, 74, 75, 81, 82, 102, 103, 104, 105, 106, 107, 111, 112*
apostles' doctrine *71*
Apostolic Church *72*
Ascension *39*

B
baptism of the Holy Ghost *5, 28, 43, 50, 51, 52, 71, 82, 83, 102, 107*
baptized into Jesus Christ *102*
baptizo *74*
Before Abraham was, I am *93*
begotten *88, 90, 97*
believe on Jesus Christ *101, 102*
biblical correction *10*
biblical doctrine *83*
biblical errors *29*
bizarre *14*
born again of water and the Spirit *102*
breaking free *54*

C
Catholic
beliefs *29*
charismatic movement *50*
doctrines *28*
faith *9, 16*
mannerisms *29*
mass *60*
nuns *32, 41, 44*
practices *16*
traditions *16*
Catholicism *19, 27, 56*
circumcision *69, 104*
confession *62, 67, 69*
conviction *13, 73, 85*
co-Redemptrix *27*

D
deeper Catholic experience *5, 16, 19*
displeasing the Lord *19, 36*

E
erroneous ideas *20*
eternal salvation *25, 111*

F
faith in Jesus Christ *73, 105*
filled with the Holy Ghost *28, 66, 73*
first pope *67, 69*
former Catholic *16, 28, 59*
former practices *18, 63*
foundation of the church *68, 69*
fully God *90, 96*
fully human *90, 96*

G
godfather *54, 55*
God incarnate *97*
God is a Spirit *84, 85, 87*
God-man *87, 90*
God manifested in human flesh *87*

godmother *55*
godparent *55*
graven image *35, 36*

H

heathen *37, 114*
Hebrew Temple *57*
Holy of Holies *58*
human logic *83*
human redemption *87, 111*

I

I AM *11, 16, 18, 22, 32, 37, 62, 65, 67, 68, 75, 93, 94, 97, 101, 107, 110, 111, 115, 117*
idolatry *19, 35, 36, 39*
idols *35*
Immanuel *76*
in the name of Jesus Christ *73, 74, 75, 81, 82, 103, 111, 112*
invisible God *95*

J

jealous God *32, 36*
Jesus is our Priest *31*
Johnstone *74, 75, 76, 77*
judgment *9, 64, 65*

L

loopholes *9*
love God's Word *117*

M

Mary's salvation *43*
mediator *30, 39, 43, 47*
Mediatrix *27, 29*
misconceptions *100, 101*
missalettes *77*
mother of God *39*
my spiritual journey *25*

O

obedience to the plan of salvation *105*
obedient faith *111, 116*
one God *30, 84, 86*
Oneness of God *83, 97, 99*
only One without sin *46*
our Mediator is Jesus *30*

P

Pentecost *43, 50, 58, 66, 72, 80, 81, 102, 105, 111, 112*
persecution *113, 114, 116, 117*
personal relationship *10, 80*
personal turmoil *53*
Petra *69*
Petros *68*
physical abuse *51*
power of God's Word *18*
prayer meetings *5, 51*
prayers of Jesus *91*
praying in front of statues *35*
praying to Mary *27, 35, 37*
purgatory *64, 65*

R

relationship with God *25, 79*
repentance *13, 14, 77, 82, 102, 104, 105, 107, 116*
Roman road to salvation *101, 104*

S

sacraments *72*
search for truth *9*
self-help *9*
siblings *41*
Son of God *31, 48, 86, 87, 89, 90, 95, 96, 97, 105*
Son of Man *90, 91*
speaking in other tongues *28, 82*
speaking in tongues *15*

Index

spirit of love **9**
spiritual explorers **22**
spiritual navigation **22**
spiritual traditions **24**
sprinkling **30**, **47**, **74**

T

tabernacle **47**, **57**, **58**, **59**, **60**, **64**, **65**
Terry **16**, **17**, **18**, **19**, **25**, **27**, **28**, **29**, **30**, **32**, **39**, **40**, **41**, **51**, **71**
the Almighty **53**, **93**, **97**, **99**
the blood of Jesus **71**
the Catholic altar **57**
the saints **32**, **33**, **35**, **37**
Trinitarian **99**
Trinity **83**, **84**, **85**, **86**, **99**, **100**
triune Godhead **83**
Truth or tradition **109**
types and shadows **59**

U

unbiblical practices **35**

V

virgin **39**, **43**, **49**, **87**, **90**
visible image **95**

SCRIPTURE INDEX

Old Testament
Exodus 3:13–14 *93*
Exodus 20:3–6 *36*
Exodus 20:5 *36*
Exodus 34:7 *45*
Exodus 34:14 *32*
Exodus 39:1–5 *61*
Exodus 39:41 *61*
Exodus 40:18–32 *60*
Deuteronomy 2:4 *85*
Deuteronomy 5:7–8 *35*
Deuteronomy 6:4–5 *85*
Psalm 19:7 *80*
Psalm 90:2; 93:2 *87*
Psalm 100:5 *23*
Psalm 119:2 *38*
Psalm 119:9–11 *24*
Psalm 119:89 *23*
Psalm 119:105 *23*
Isaiah 9:6 *77*
Isaiah 41:21 *37*
Isaiah 42:6–8 *32*
Isaiah 43:3 *97*
Isaiah 43:11 *48*, *97*
Hosea 4:6 *63*
Hosea 13:4 *97*

New Testament
Matthew 1:18 *46*, *87*, *90*
Matthew 1:21 *49*, *76*, *103*
Matthew 1:21–23 *49*
Matthew 1:24–25 *40*
Matthew 4:1–11 *91*
Matthew 6:7 *37*
Matthew 7:21–23 *64*
Matthew 10:22 *116*
Matthew 10:32–39 *116*
Matthew 10:37 *53*
Matthew 12:25–26 *80*
Matthew 12:47–50 *41*
Matthew 13:55–56 *40*, *41*
Matthew 16:15–19 *67*
Matthew 27:46 *98*
Matthew 27:50–51 *57*
Matthew 28:18 *96*
Matthew 28:19 *75*, *76*
Mark 3:31–32 *40*, *41*
Mark 7:13 *24*
Mark 10:15 *80*
Luke 1:30–33 *49*
Luke 1:35 *87*
Luke 1:45 *49*
Luke 1:46–47 *48*
Luke 9:22 *91*
Luke 10:21–22 *92*
Luke 22:41–42 *91*
Luke 24:45–47 *78*
Luke 24:49 *87*
John 1:1–18 *88*
John 2:1–5 *33*
John 2:19–21 *98*
John 3:5 *102*
John 4:21–24 *85*
John 5:39 *23*
John 5:43 *75*, *76*
John 8:1–59 *92*
John 8:31–32 *62*
John 10:23–31 *93*
John 14:6 *22*, *110*
John 14:8–9 *75*
John 14:8–10 *94*
John 14:9 *88*
John 14:13–14 *38*
John 14:26 *75*, *76*, *87*
John 16:13 *5*, *112*
John 16:23–24 *31*

Scripture Index

John 16:33 **113**
John 17:17 **43**, **109**
John 18:38 **22**
John 19:34 **77**
Acts 1:8 **81**, **87**, **112**
Acts 1:8, 13–15; 2:1–4, 12–40 **87**
Acts 1:13–14 **50**
Acts 2:1–4 **66**, **112**
Acts 2:14–39 **73**
Acts 2:38–40 **111**
Acts 11:26 **70**
Acts 19:1–6 **103**
Acts 22:16 **112**
Romans 3:4 **110**
Romans 3:12 **44**
Romans 3:22–26 **45**
Romans 4:9 **102**
Romans 5:12 **46**
Romans 6:1–2 **103**
Romans 6:3 **102**
Romans 8:35–39 **117**
Romans 10:9 **101**, **103**, **104**, **105**
Romans 11 **105**
Romans 14:12 **63**
Romans 14:17 **81**
I Corinthians 1:19–21 **80**
I Corinthians 3:16 **65**
I Corinthians 10:4 **68**, **69**
I Corinthians 10:13 **114**
I Corinthians 14:23–25 **15**
I Corinthians 15:1–2 **117**
II Corinthians 1:22; 5:5 **112**
II Corinthians 4:16–18 **115**
II Corinthians 5:17–21 **47**
II Corinthians 11:24–27 **114**
Galatians 1:6–7 **19**
Galatians 1:8 **44**
Galatians 2:7–8 **70**
Galatians 5:22–24 **82**
Ephesians 1:14 **112**
Ephesians 3:15 **9**
Ephesians 4:30 **82**
Philippians 1:21–25 **115**
Philippians 2:12 **63**
Colossians 1:13–19 **95**, **96**
Colossians 1:15 **95**
Colossians 1:19; 2:8–10 **89**
I Thessalonians 2:13 **109**
I Timothy 2:5 **30**
I Timothy 3:16 **46**
II Timothy 2:15 **25**, **109**
II Timothy 3:16 **23**
Titus 1:2 **110**
Hebrews 1:1–3 **88**
Hebrews 1:3 **95**
Hebrews 1:10–12; 13:8 **87**
Hebrews 4:12 **18**
Hebrews 4:14 **31**
Hebrews 4:15 **91**
Hebrews 7:22–25 **31**
Hebrews 8:1–2, 13 **64**
Hebrews 8:5 **57**
Hebrews 8–9 **60**
Hebrews 8:10–11 **52**
Hebrews 8:13–9:5 **58**
Hebrews 9:11–15 **47**
Hebrews 9:24–28 **65**
Hebrews 9:27 **64**
Hebrews 10:16–18 **62**
Hebrews 12:5–8 **16**
Hebrews 12:24 **30**
James 2:19 **86**
I Peter 1:8 **81**
I Peter 1:18–21 **47**
I Peter 1:23–25 **23**
I Peter 2:21–22 **46**
II Peter 1:13–15 **65**
I John 1:9 **62**
I John 5:6 **110**
Revelation 1:8 **87**
Revelation 12:11 **71**, **77**
Revelation 13:8 **98**

BOOK ORDER FORM

Come Unto ME

http://www.rlmontgomery.net

Paperback books may be purchased from the author's website at: http://www.rlmontgomery.net/ with the use of a pay pal account. However, if a payment method by check or money order is preferred, paperback books may be ordered by mail with this form.

Please print clearly:

Name: _____

Address: _____

City: _____ State: _____

Zip: _____

Phone: _____

_____ copies of book at $9.95 each: $ _____

Subtotal: $ _____

OK residents add 9% sales tax: $ _____

Shipping in continental U.S. $3.50 ea book: $ _____

Total amount enclosed: $ _____

Make checks or money orders payable to:
R.L. Montgomery

Mail order to:
R.L. Montgomery
P.O. Box 368
Foyil, OK 74031